Contents

Contents continued

TECHNOLOGY

How to use this book

Scientists, techies, engineers and mathematicians all use journals to keep track of the projects they work on.

Journals are a great space to keep fascinating data from experiments, amazing ideas for new inventions, puzzling questions about why (or how or what or when) along with notes, sketches and doodles.

Project pages

Each project begins with a **question**.
Which is how people have always begun when making something new.

- ★ *How can I make my own fire?*
- ★ *How can I send a funny picture to my best friend… on another planet?*

There's a **photograph** (to save a thousand words) and some information about the topic; often interesting facts!

To get started on the project, there's a **picture list of things you'll need**. Not everything is listed but all the essentials should be there.

Now comes the fun bit!

1 There are **four steps** to each project. At least, there are four boxes.	2 Not everything is explained. Sometimes it's because there's not enough space.
3 Sometimes it's because you can tell what comes next from the pictures.	4 And sometimes, it's so you can work it out for yourself.

On the **journal page**, you'll see lots of different things:

1. Space to write about your project.
2. Space to sketch out your own ideas.
3. Charts to complete with data from your experiments.
4. More step-by-steps to take your project further.
5. Interesting facts and trivia about the subject.
6. Questions to make you think.

CHALLENGE

Challenge units
are trickier than the others

Keeping safe

Please remember to keep safe while you are working. You should know not to run with scissors and that hot things (such as a hot glue gun and irons) are well, hot!

But just so you don't forget, there are yellow safety signs on those bits that you need to be careful with; such as scissors and wire and hot glue guns…

SNERRGM tester

How can we tell if something is alive?

Everything on Earth can be classified as Alive, Used to be Alive or Non-Living. Living things have Sensitivity to their environments, need Nutrition, Excrete waste, Respire (breathe), Reproduce, Grow and Move.

What you need

A3 paper

compass

sticky notes

pictures

1 Write 'SNERRGM Tester' at the top of your paper. Use a compass to draw a large circle in the centre.  	**2** Write each characteristic on a separate sticky note and place the sticky notes around the circle. 
3 Draw, cut out or print off pictures of things that are alive, used to be alive or are non-living. 	**4** Place a picture in the circle and decide how many characteristics it has. Remove the ones that cannot be observed. 

1 Earth has sent a robotic rover to Mars. Would the Martians think the rover is alive? Use your SNERRGM tester then complete the chart below.

Characteristic	How could they tell?	Characteristic	How could they tell?
Sensitivity		Reproduction	
Nutrition		Growth	
Excretion		Movement	
Respiration			

2 Earth sends astronauts in spacesuits to Mars. Could the Martians tell if *they* were living things? Use your SNERRGM tester then complete the chart.

Characteristic	How could they tell?	Characteristic	How could they tell?
Sensitivity		Reproduction	
Nutrition		Growth	
Excretion		Movement	
Respiration			

3 The Martian sitting on the rock decides to say hello to the astronauts. How could the Earth visitors decide if the *Martian* was actually alive? Use your SNERRGM tester then complete the chart.

Characteristic	How could they tell?	Characteristic	How could they tell?
Sensitivity		Reproduction	
Nutrition		Growth	
Excretion		Movement	
Respiration			

IS THERE LIFE ON MARS?

- To date, there is no proof that there is or has been life on Mars.
- There was liquid on the surface a long time ago that could have supported micro-organisms.
- The European spacecraft *ExoLander* and the US *Mars 2020* rover will explore Mars for signs of life in 2020.

TARGETING STEM JOURNAL 4 @ PASCAL PRESS ISBN 9781925726091

Frog habitats

How can we make a habitat for tadpoles and frogs?

Humans have different needs as babies and as adults. Frogs have different needs as eggs and as tadpoles or adults. A good habitat will provide for the needs of the frog at each stage of the life cycle allowing movement, growth and respiration.

SCIENCE SSU072, SSU073, SSU074, SHE061, SIS065, SIS071

MATHEMATICS MMG084, MMG290, MMG090

What you need

foam sheet

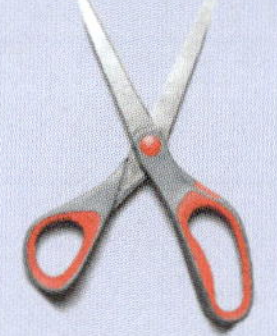

sharp knife, scissors

rocks, weights, wire

large ice-cream container and lid

1 Complete the Journal activities first. Draw the five life cycle stages on the plastic lid and cut out.

2 Make an island from the foam sheet. Make sloping edges for the frogs to lie in or climb on.

3 Fill the container with water. Add the foam island and adapt it to float in the water. Add rocks on top for shelter.

4 Add your life cycle cut-outs under and *in* the water and on the island. Review your design.

TARGETING STEM JOURNAL 4 @ PASCAL PRESS ISBN 9781925726091

1 Label the life cycle diagram. Use these words: adult frog, tadpole, tadpole with two legs, tadpole with four legs, eggs.

2 The frog's needs change through the life cycle. Sketch out a design for an aquarium habitat that has a place for:

- eggs and tadpoles to be completely in the water.
- tadpoles with legs to rest but still be in shallow water.
- adult frogs to be sheltered on land but with easy access in and out of the water.

3 Foam floats well but on top of the water rather than in it. Think of some ways you could make foam float *in* the water. How could you shape it to make it easier for frogs to get on and off?

IMPORTANT NOTE ABOUT FROGS

! Don't test your habitat with real frogs because there are laws in Australia about keeping frogs. Contact your education department to find out if you can collect frogs' eggs or tadpoles. Your state may have a special licence for schools to keep frogs, but there are strict guidelines on the types of frogs and the number of tadpoles that can be collected.

Frog websites

frogs.org.au/frogs/

australianmuseum.net.au/learn/animals/frogs/

Seed dispersal

How can we adapt a bean seed to disperse through the air?

Plants reproduce by spreading their seeds. This can happen in several different ways. Seeds may spin or glide through the air, be carried by animals in their food or fur. Some seed pods float in water, others even explode spreading the seeds a long distance from the plant.

What you need

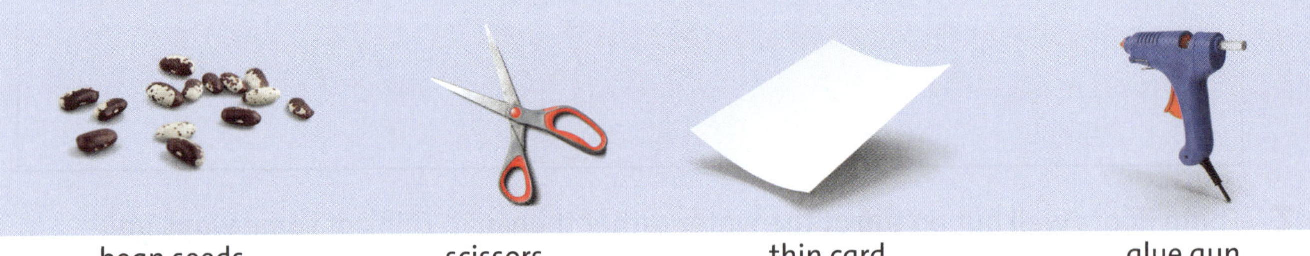

bean seeds | scissors | thin card | glue gun

1 Cut out four wings from light card for the bean seed. Use the main picture as a guide.

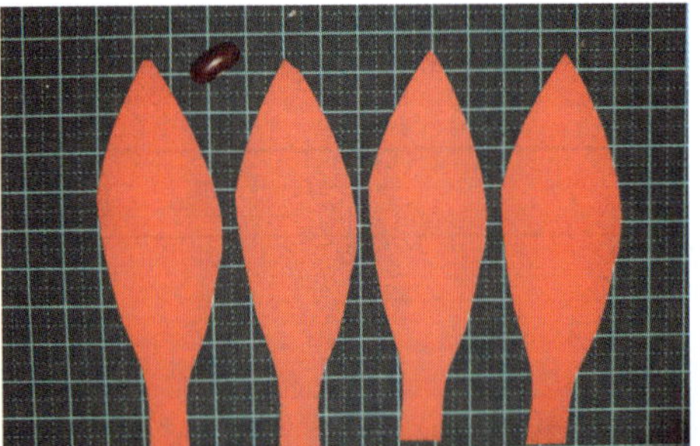

2 Pull the wings carefully and gently over the back of a pair of scissors to curve them.

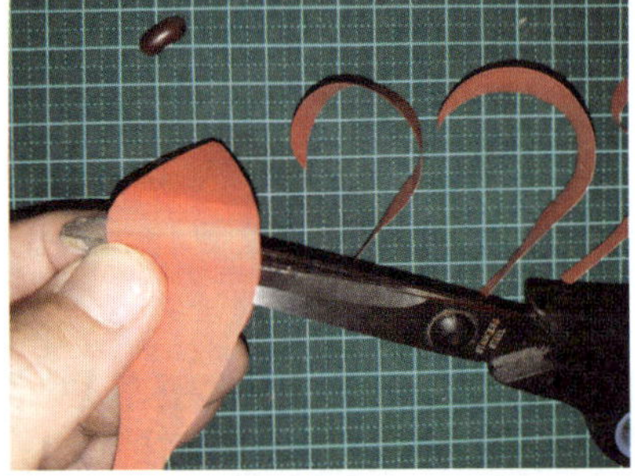

3 Stick the four wings onto the bean seed.

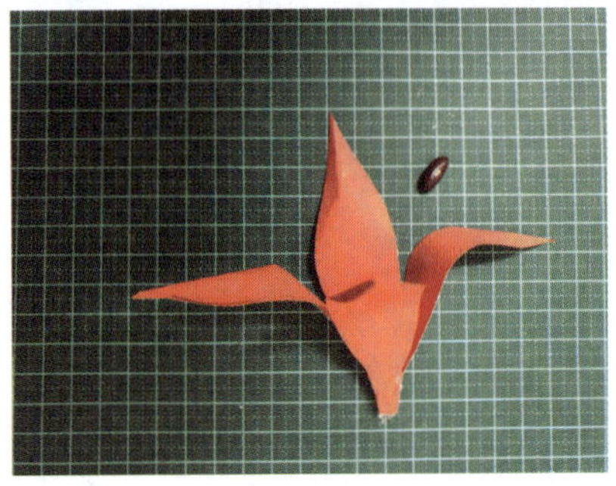

4 Drop the 'flying bean' from head height to see how far it travels.

TARGETING STEM JOURNAL 4 @ PASCAL PRESS ISBN 9781925726091

1 Record the results of your test flight below. What did the bean do as it fell? How far did the bean travel horizontally? What happened when it landed? How could you improve the 'flying bean'?

___

___

___

2 Look at the pictures below. Write how you think each seed travels away from the plant. Use the words: float in water, float through the air, stick to an animal, spin through the air.

3 How else could you adapt a bean seed to travel away from its plant? Think about adding sails, spikes or flotation devices. Design your new seed below using only organic materials.

4 Test your seed using the criteria below.

Dispersal Type	Flying	Sticking	Floating
Criteria	**Travel through the air for at least 2m**	**Stick to an animal and travel at least 5m**	**Float in water for at least 10 minutes**
Your seed design			

SEED DISPERSAL BY HUMANS

Humans also disperse seeds:

- On their clothes and shoes (up to 5km)
- By cars and other vehicles (over 100km)
- Deliberately by dropping mud balls containing seeds or by 'seed bombing' from aircraft to quickly reseed a burned-out area.

TARGETING STEM JOURNAL 4 @ PASCAL PRESS ISBN 9781925726091

Butterfly feeder

Adult butterflies generally take nectar from flowers for nutrition. They suck up the nectar through a little pipe. They also suck up water and mushy foods such as soft bananas, juicy oranges or watermelon.

What you need

waterproof plate | string and a flat rock | hammer and nail | fruit pieces

1 Punch four holes in the waterproof plate.

2 Attach string through the holes. Tie the ends together.

3 Hot glue a flat rock to the centre for stability.

4 Hang the plate outside in a sheltered position. Add a little water.

TARGETING STEM JOURNAL 4 @ PASCAL PRESS ISBN 9781925726091

1 Butterflies feed on juicy, sticky nectar from flowers. What foods could you add to your feeder to attract butterflies? Look at the suggestions in the information box. Test them out on your feeder. Record the number of butterflies that visit each food.

Banana	Orange	Watermelon

2 Butterflies are attracted to colourful flowers. Make some artificial flowers for your feeder. Use brightly coloured paper and attach them around the edge. Test some of these questions:

- Is the size of your flowers important? Test large and small 'flowers'.
- Is the shape of your flowers important? Test triangles and squares 'flowers'.
- Do your flowers need to 'smell'? Add a little juice to the surface of your 'flowers'.

Record your results below.

____

____

____

____

____

____

BUTTERFLY-CAM

If it's difficult to observe your feeder during the day, consider setting up a tablet nearby. Most camera apps have a setting for taking photos at intervals. That way you can check in on your butterfly guests even when you're not there.

Other insects may be attracted to your butterfly feeder, such as bees and wasps. Take care if unwelcome guests appear.

TARGETING STEM JOURNAL 4 @ PASCAL PRESS ISBN 9781925726091

CHALLENGE

UV bee vision

How can we model what a bee sees?

Humans have three photoreceptors in their eyes that are sensitive to the colours red, blue and green. Bees also have three photoreceptors but their photoreceptors are sensitive to blue, green and UV (ultraviolet) light. So what a bee and a human see when they look at a flower is very different.

What you need

blue and purple permanent marker pens

sticky tape

LED light

fluorescent markers

1 Place a piece of sticky tape over the LED light. Colour the tape blue.

2 Place a second piece of sticky tape over the first. Colour the tape blue.

3 Place a third piece of sticky tape over the other two. Colour it purple.

4 Write on paper with the marker. Shine the LED light on it in a dark room.

TARGETING STEM JOURNAL 4 @ PASCAL PRESS ISBN 9781925726091

1 Pick some flowers from the garden. Make colour sketches of them in normal and in blue-purple light.

	Flower 1	Flower 2	Flower 3	Flower 4
Normal light				
Blue/purple light				

2 Optical brighteners are chemicals added to materials to make them look brighter. Paper, cosmetics and washing powders all have optical brighteners in them. In a darkened room, shine your blue-purple light on the items below. Record your observations.

white socks   high-vis vest   blank paper

3 Try testing a bank note with your blue-purple light. Does it glow? How could that information help if you were checking for fake notes?

4 Test the pages of a new library book. Now find a library book that was published at least 10 years (or more) ago. What do you notice? Why do you think there is a difference?

New Book	Old Book

CHALLENGE

Stop-motion life cycle

How can we animate a life cycle in plasticine?

In stop-motion animation, an object is moved then photographed in its new position. If the photos are played back quickly, the object will appear to move. Clay-mation is stop-motion animation using plasticine.

What you need

tablet and stop motion app

stand to support the tablet

plasticine or modelling clay

plain background

1 Complete Journal section 1. Make models of the stages of the life cycle.

2 Film the first section. Move the model in small steps, no more than 2mm each time. Take at least 50 pictures.

3 Repeat for the other sections. Remember: small movements and lots of them!

4 Play back your animation.

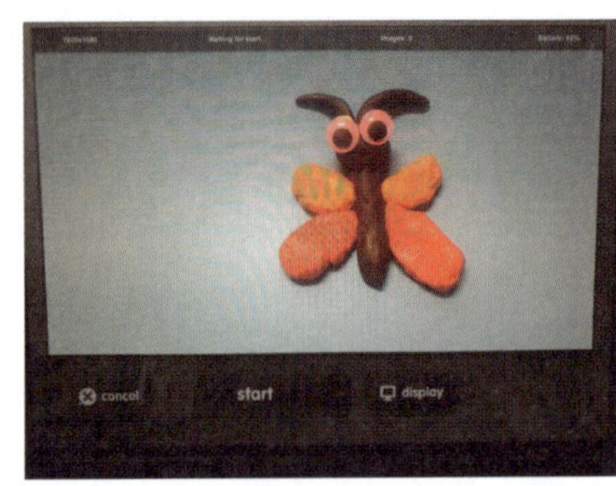

1 Decide which life cycle you will animate then sketch out the stages below. Use the frog life cycle from Unit 2, the butterfly life cycle below, the sunflower life cycle from unit 7 or your own research for ideas.

Scene 1	Scene 2	Scene 3	Scene 4

ANIMATION IDEAS

- Animate titles for your film by writing then photographing the letters one by one.
- Use natural materials alongside your plasticine models. For example, you could use real grass, leaves or flowers.
- Your stop-motion was filmed with one scene for each stage in the life cycle. In real life animals and insects change bit by bit from one stage to another. Remake the film with your model showing the changes. For example, your tadpole could grow legs or your caterpillar could weave a cocoon.

STOP-MOTION AT THE MOVIES

- The first record of stop-motion was back in 1897 in the film *The Humpty Dumpty Circus.*
- Stop-motion was used in 1933 to animate *King Kong*.
- The chess game in the first *Star Wars* film was made using stop -motion.
- *The Adventures of Wallace and Gromit* is the highest grossing stop-motion movie.

Growing sunflowers

Do all sunflower seeds take the same time to germinate?

Germination is the process by which a plant grows from a seed. Different plants have different germination times. For example, some beans can germinate in just 10 days while asparagus can take up to 35 days.

What you need

plastic tray

seed raising mixture

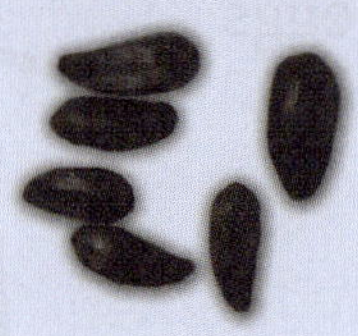

sunflower seeds

1 Complete the first Journal section. Fill the seed tray with seed raising mixture.

2 Follow the instructions on the packet to plant the seeds.

3 Keep the seeds damp and in a warm place.

4 Check the seeds each day. Record the number of germinated seeds.

TARGETING STEM JOURNAL 4 @ PASCAL PRESS ISBN 9781925726091

1 Look at the life cycle below. Which stage will you use as the guide for deciding if your sunflower has germinated? Circle that stage and explain why.

2 Record on the graph the number of seeds that have germinated each day. (Spoiler alert – don't expect to see much before six days!)

Day	1	2	3	4	5	6	7	8	9	10	11	12	13	14	15

3 Did all seeds germinate on the same day? What advantages or disadvantages would this have for the seed's survival?

____

____

____

____

GERMINATION RECORDS

- In 2008, a palm plant sprouted from a seed nearly 2000 years old.
- A few years later seeds found buried in permafrost by a squirrel were germinated. They were 32,00 years old!

- Read all the instructions on the seed raising mixture.
- Wear gloves when handling the mixture.

TARGETING STEM JOURNAL 4 @ PASCAL PRESS ISBN 9781925726091

CHALLENGE

Dirty water

Are decaying plants bad for fish?

Fish have gills to breathe in the oxygen contained in water. Aquarium owners will remove uneaten food or dead fish as they can use up oxygen as they decay. The chemical mixture Bromothymol blue is used to check the oxygen levels.

What you need

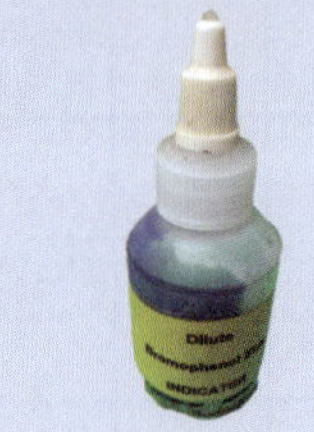

Bromothymol blue

2 small glass jars

leaves

water

1 Fill the two jars with water to the same level.

2 Add 20 drops of Bromothymol blue to each jar.

3 Add leaves to the top of one jar. Keep the other as your control.

4 Seal the jars and observe for five days.

1 Keep a record of the changes you observe in each jar.

	Day 1	Day 2	Day 3	Day 4	Day 5
Jar 1: Leaves					
Jar 2: Control					

2 Bromothymol blue changes from blue to yellow as oxygen in the water is used up. Which jar was more yellow? Why do you think this was?

3 Why do you think environmentalists are concerned about leaves washing into our streams and rivers in autumn?

4 Leaves that blow into gutters and street kerbs are often washed into stormwater drains and out into rivers or the sea. Do a kerbside leaf survey in autumn to see how big the problem could be.

- Mark out a 50m stretch of curb that has leaves.
- Collect the leaves into recyclable plastic bags.
- Calculate how many bags you would collect on a 1km stretch.
- Dispose of the leaves in a green bin or onto a compost heap.

Making slime

What you need

½ cup thick shampoo
1-2 cups of cornflour
food colouring and water

Ingredients | mixing bowl | spoon

1 Mix ½ cup of shampoo with a ¼ cup of cornflour.

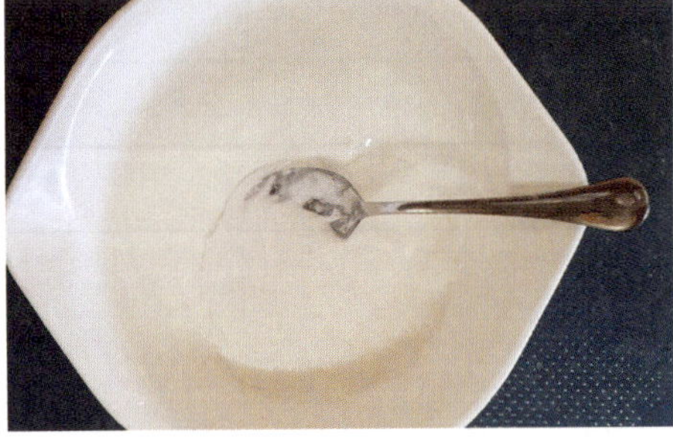

2 Add 3-4 drops of food colouring.

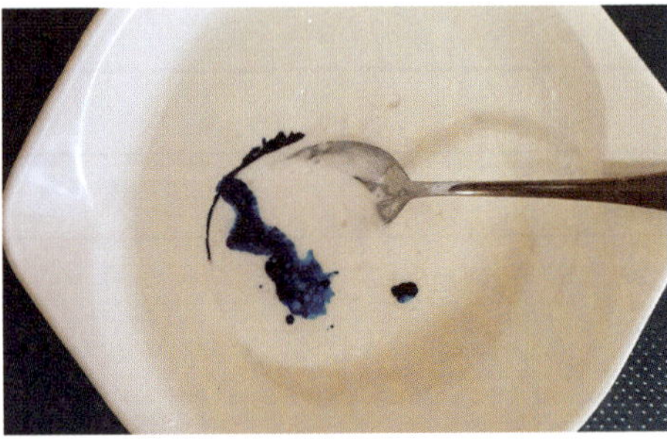

3 Add 1 tbsp of water and ¼ cup of cornflour and mix. Write your observations in the table in Journal 1.

4 Repeat step 3 until the slime is the right consistency.

TARGETING STEM JOURNAL 4 @ PASCAL PRESS ISBN 9781925726091

1 The exact amount of cornflour you'll need to add will depend on your shampoo. After the first cup of cornflour (step 3) draw on the arrow to show how close to being slime your mixture is. Write a sentence in the notes column about what you observe each time.

Cornflour	too slimy <-> too dry	Notes
¼ cup	⟷	
2 × ¼ cups	⟷	
3 × ¼ cups	⟷	
4 × ¼ cups	⟷	

2 How could you test your slime for stretchiness? (Ideas: Pull the slime along a table. Pull down through the air. Pull from one desk to another.) Design and draw an experiment below.

____

____

____

3 Divide your slime into three equal pieces. Conduct your experiment on piece 1 and record the results below. Run warm water over piece 2, knead and repeat the experiment. Mix some cornflour with piece 3, knead and repeat the experiment.

Experiment	Stretch distance before breaking	Observations
1 – control piece		
2 – with warm water		
3 – with extra cornflour		

SLIME NOTES

- Keep the slime in an airtight container when not in use.
- Throw your slime away if it gets mouldy!
- Teachers: It's a good idea to test the ingredients you provide students as not all brands o f shampoo will mix in the same way.

SLIME SAFETY

Many slime recipes include the ingredient 'borax' or sodium borate. This has been known to irritate sensitive skin. This recipe uses shampoo and cornflour instead and although not as shiny as traditional slime it should be safer.

TARGETING STEM JOURNAL 4 @ PASCAL PRESS ISBN 9781925726091

10 The best play dough recipe

How can we decide which recipe makes the best play dough?

Play dough is a popular activity for younger children who enjoy touching, squashing and modelling the soft material. Many people make their own play dough and there are lots of 'best' recipes on the Internet.

SIS085

What you need

2 cups plain flour
1 cup salt
4 tsp cream of tartar
2 tbsp cooking oil
2 cups warm water

Ingredients

Saucepan

Bowl

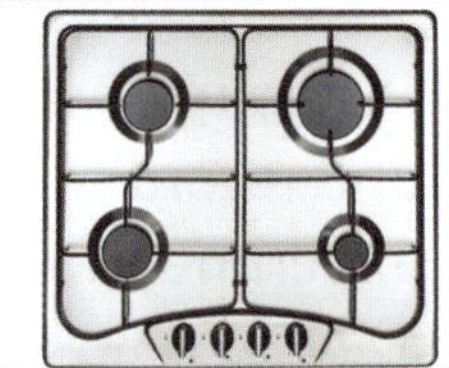

Cooktop

1 Sift the dry ingredients together into a large saucepan.

MMG290

2 Add the oil and warm water. Mix together over low heat until the dough thickens.

3 Remove from the saucepan and let it cool.

4 Knead the dough until it is smooth.

SCIENCE SSU074, SHE061, SIS065, SIS068, SIS071

MATHEMATICS MMG084, MMG290

TARGETING STEM JOURNAL 4 @ PASCAL PRESS ISBN 9781925726091

1 The play dough you made was on an Internet page that claimed it was the 'best recipe'. Rate the play dough you made:

	🙂	😐	🙁	Comments
Easy to find ingredients				
Simple to follow recipe				
Soft and not too crumby				
Bright colours				
Pleasant smell				

2 These are the ingredients for a different 'best play dough' recipe. What differences can you see between the two recipes?

- 2 cups plain flour
- ½ cup salt
- 2 tbsp cream of tartar
- 2 tbsp cooking oil
- 1 ½ cups very hot water

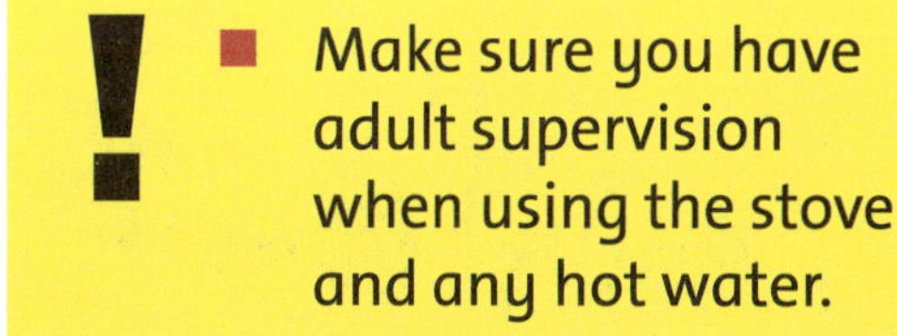

Under adult supervision, make a batch of the second play dough. Rate it below:

	🙂	😐	🙁	Comments
Easy to find ingredients				
Simple to follow recipe				
Soft and not too crumby				
Bright colours				
Pleasant smell				

3 Being 'best' depends on what aspect of the product you think is important. Complete the 'best play dough' chart below:

	Recipe 1	Recipe 2
Best to make with little children		
Best to make models from		
Best to squish and squeeze		
Best to wash off hands afterwards		

4 Neither of the recipes includes instructions for colouring the play dough. Do an Internet search for making play dough and research when colouring should be added. Make a batch of coloured play dough using either of the 'best' recipes.

Plastic from milk

How can we make plastic toys from milk?

Casein plastic was discovered over 100 years ago by a scientist trying to make waterproof coating. It was used to make small items such as buttons, pen handles and knitting needles.

What you need

1 cup milk
4 tbsp vinegar

Ingredients

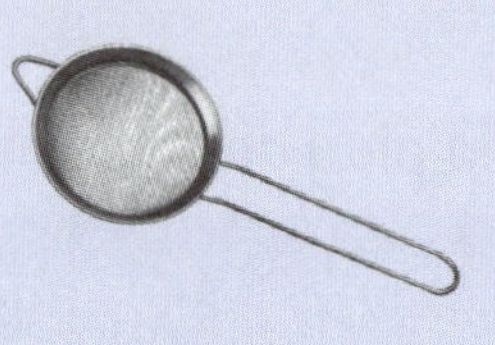

sieve

paper towels

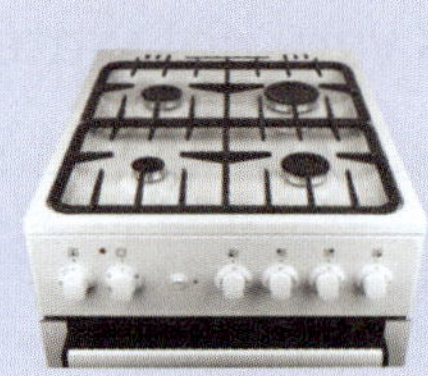

stove and saucepan

1 Gently heat a cup of milk until it is steaming.

2 Remove from the heat and stir in four tablespoons of vinegar.

3 Strain the mixture through a sieve.

4 Pat the mixture with paper towels to absorb any remaining liquid.

1 Make a simple plastic toy by using your plastic in a mould:

a. Shape plasticine into a thick block and press a toy into it.

b. Carefully remove the toy and fill the space with the casein plastic.

c. Leave the plastic to set over 2-3 days, then carefully remove the plasticine.

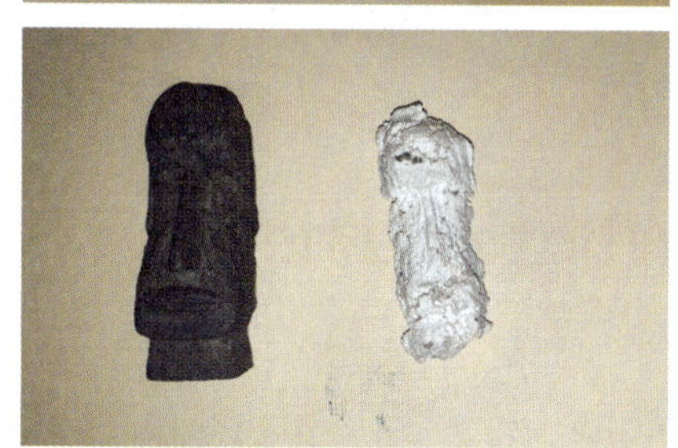

2 The casein plastic is formed by a chemical reaction between the casein in the milk and the acid in the vinegar. Other dairy products such as cream also contain casein and fruit juices can be acidic too. Experiment with some combinations and record your results.

Dairy products: low fat milk, full fat milk, cream
Acidic juices: lemon juice, orange juice, pineapple juice

Dairy product +	Acidic juice	What did your casein plastic look like?

- Take care when heating the milk on the stove – have an adult nearby.
- Remove the saucepan when the milk is just beginning to steam. Do not let it boil!
- For a safer alternative, heat the milk in a microwave for around 30 seconds.
- Teachers: It is best to test the ingredients you will use with the students as not all cornflour products will react in the same way.

Electric paint

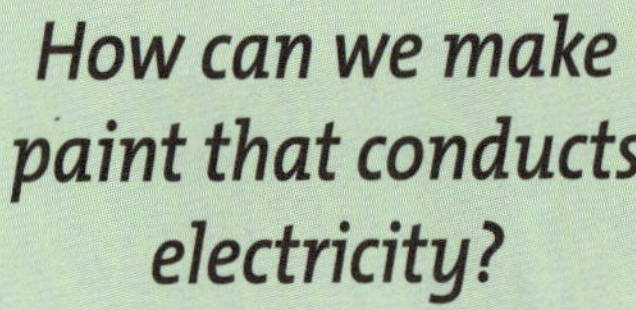

How can we make paint that conducts electricity?

Graphite is a crystal form of carbon. It is used in pencils and as a dry lubricant. Because it conducts electricity, it is also used in batteries, for motor brushes (in the photo) and solar panels.

What you need

PVA glue
graphite powder

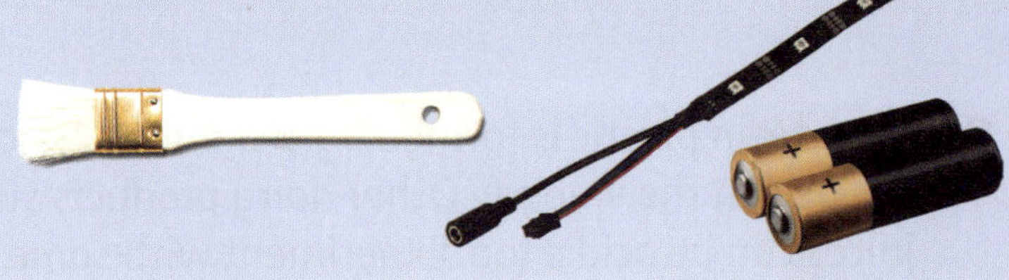

Ingredients | disposable mixing container | brush | LED, battery and wires

1 Pour in enough white glue to cover the bottom of the tray.

2 Mix in a heaped tablespoon of graphite powder.

3 Add and mix more graphite until the mixture is thick, gritty but still flows a little.

4 Use the brush to paint a line on card.

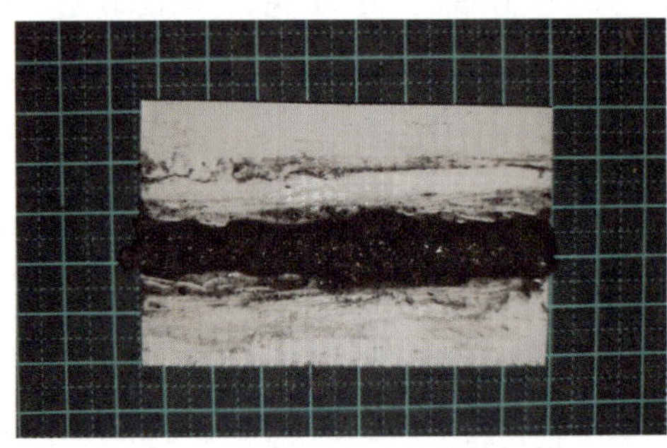

TARGETING STEM JOURNAL 4 @ PASCAL PRESS ISBN 9781925726091

1 To test your electric paint, you'll need an LED and a battery and your test card.

  a. Press the black LED lead onto the paint. Hold it in place with a rubber band.
  b. Connect the positive lead of the LED to the battery.
  c. Connect a spare piece of wire to the negative side of the battery.
  d. Touch the paint in different places to see if the LED glows.

2 How could you make a switch for your electric paint circuit? For example, you could make a section of the circuit rotate with split pins. Sketch out your design below then construct it.

TRANSPARENT GRAPHITE

Graphene is a very thin layer of graphite, just one atom thick! It is the strongest material so far discovered and can be used to make other materials stronger. It is also transparent and conducts electricity. It can be used in solar panels, touchscreens, water filters and batteries.

- Powdered graphite is very fine, so avoid spilling or inhaling the particles.
- Teachers: Test the recipe before trying with students. The mixture should be quite gritty.

Bungy jumping

How can we make a doll safely bungy jump from the door?

Bungy (or bungee) jumping involves jumping from a tall structure while attached to an elastic cord. The cord stretches as the person free falls then contracts and the jumper flies upward again.

What you need

30 cm plastic doll

elastic bands

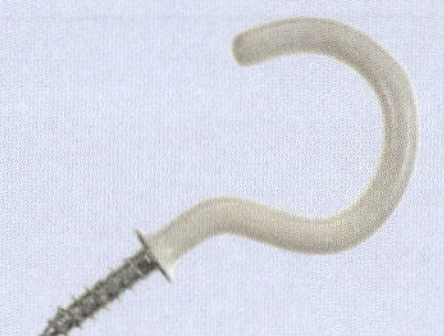

doorway and hook

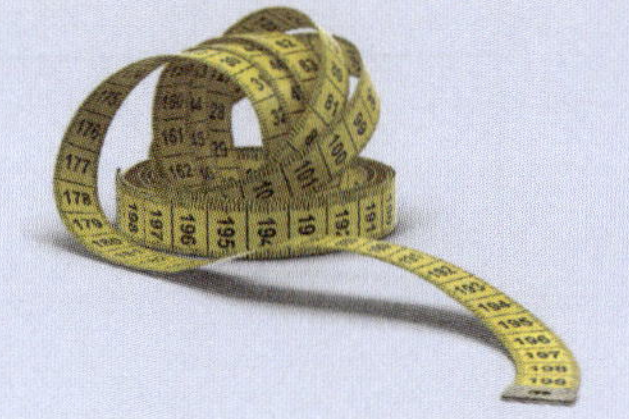

tape measure

1 Make a bungy cord by joining the elastic bands together to make a cord about half as long as the door height.

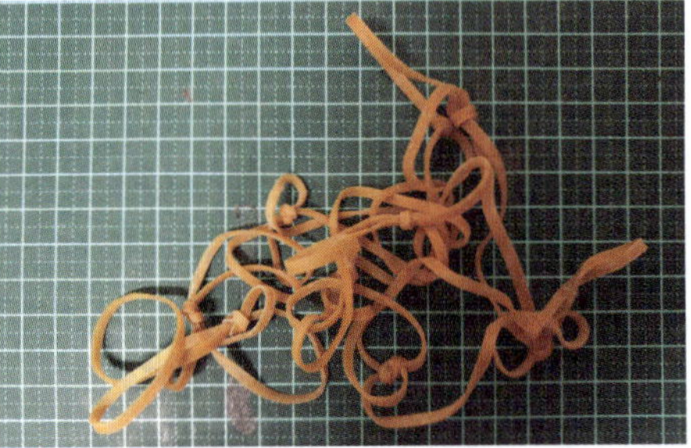

2 Attach the bungy cord securely to the doll's feet.

3 Attach the other end of the bungy cord to the top of the door frame. You may need to use the hook.

4 Stand on a chair and release the doll from the top of door. Record the results of the bungy jump in the Journal.

TARGETING STEM JOURNAL 4 @ PASCAL PRESS ISBN 9781925726091

1 The aim of bungy jumping is for the cord to stretch enough so that the person (or doll) *just* misses the ground. In the space below, record the number of elastic bands you used and the length of the unstretched cord. Record how the jump went:

- The doll hit the ground FAIL
- The doll missed the ground by more than 5 cm FAIL
- The doll got within 5 cm without hitting PASS

Experiment No.	No. of elastic bands	Length (cm)	Result of jump
1			☐ FAIL ☐ PASS

2 Look at your results from Step 1. Do you need to add more elastic bands or remove some? Complete the chart below and test your guess. Repeat until you can reliably have your doll bungy jump to within 5 cm of the floor.

Experiment No.	No. of elastic bands	Length (cm)	Result of jump
2			☐ FAIL ☐ PASS
3			☐ FAIL ☐ PASS
4			☐ FAIL ☐ PASS

3 Experiment with other designs of bungy cords. Write the results below.

- Use thicker / wider / stronger rubber bands.
- Use elastic.
- Plait three bungy cords together.

____

____

____

BUNGY RECORDS

- The first modern bungy jump was made on April 1, 1979 from the 76 m high Clifton Suspension Bridge in the UK.
- The "Highest Commercial Bungee Jump in the World" is 223 m from the Macau Tower in China.
- *Bungy Running* is done on a horizontal surface, with a cord attached to a runner's back.

CHALLENGE

14 Roof construction

How can we build a roof suitable for a tropical environment?

House roofs vary considerably around the world. Some climates will need the roof to provide shade, while others will need shelter from rain. Roof designs will also change according to what materials are available or when the house was constructed.

SCIENCE SSU074

What you need

cardboard, glue, sticky tape

natural materials

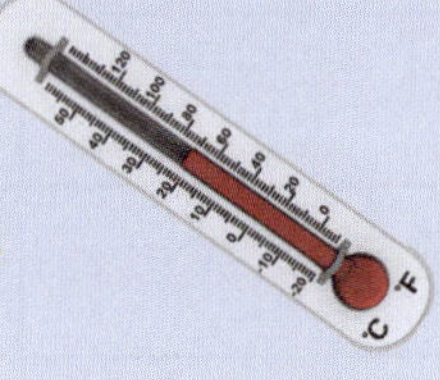

thermometer and lamp

fan

watering can

1 Build a simple house frame from card.

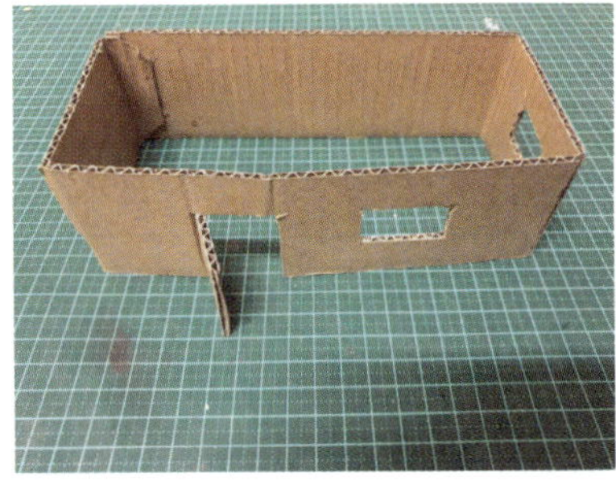

2 Cut out a rectangular flat roof that just overhangs the sides of the house.

3 Complete the three tests on the Journal page.

4 Make a new roof for the house based on the 'information in the 'Apia (Samoa)' panel. Redo the three tests with the new roof.

MATHEMATICS MMG084, MMG087

TARGETING STEM JOURNAL 4 @ PASCAL PRESS ISBN 9781925726091

1 Average temperature in the tropics is high. **A good roof will keep the inside of the house cool and provide shade around the outside.** Test your roof by placing a thermometer inside the house and positioning a lamp above. Record the temperature every minute for 10 minutes.

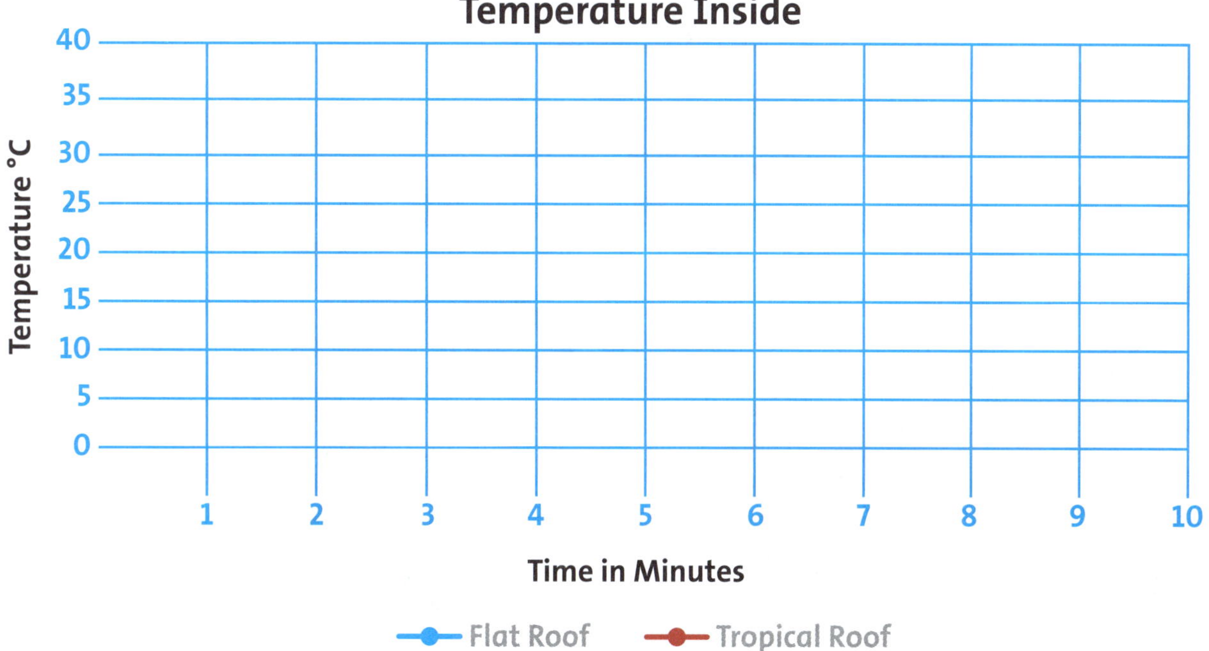

2 Average rainfall in the tropics is high. **A good roof will keep the inside of the house dry and allow rain to run off.** Test your roof by slowly pouring half a cup of water onto it. Record how much water gets inside and the condition of the roof afterwards.

Roof type	Amount of 'rain" inside	'Rain' runs off	Condition of roof after 'rain'
Flat			
Tropical			

3 Wind speeds can gust very high in tropical storms. **A good roof will be shaped so that it stays on the building in a storm.** Test your roof by blowing air from a fan at it. Record the results from the fans speed settings.

Roof type	Low speed	Medium speed	High speed
Flat			
Tropical			

APIA, (SAMOA) INFORMATION

Apia is the capital of Samoa. It has an average monthly temperature of 26 °C compared to around 15 °C for Melbourne so shade around the house is very important. It has an average rainfall of 3317 mm (over 3 m!) compared to 666 mm for Melbourne so traditional houses often have steep, thick roofs made of natural materials to keep the rain out. Apia has been hit by cyclones with winds of over 160 kph recorded.

Clay + silt + sand = soil

How can we classify a soil?

Soils are made up of differing amounts of clay, silt and sand. How much a soil contains of these determines its classification as a clay soil, a loam soil or a sandy soil. Farmers use soil texture classification to check that soils are suitable for planting particular crops.

What you need

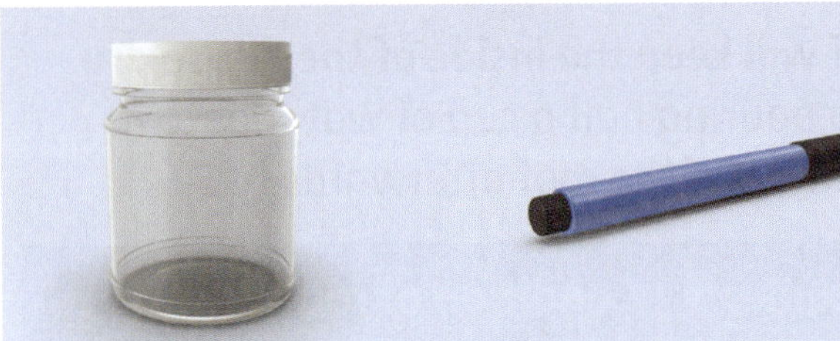

large glass jar with lid

marker pen

soil samples

water

1 Fill the jar half way with soil.

2 Add enough water to make the soil muddy.

3 Mark the top of the soil (A). Record this in the Journal section.

4 Fill the jar almost to the top with water. Put the lid on.

1 Shake the jar until the soil is mixed in with the water. Put the jar down and let it settle for a minute. Mark the new level on the jar (B) and record the height. Let the soil mixture in the jar settle for another five hours. Mark the new level on the jar (C) and record the height.

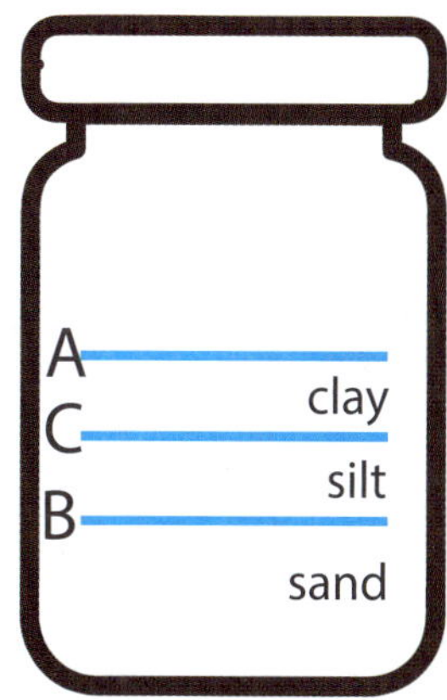

Height from bottom of jar:	Soil Sample 1	Soil sample 2
A: At start		
B: After one minute		
C: After 5 hours		

2 Calculate the amount of sand, clay and silt in your sample.

- The amount of sand is height B.
- The amount of clay is height A minus height C.
- The amount of silt is height C minus height B.

	Calculation	Soil Sample 1	Soil sample 2
Sand	**Height B**		
Clay	**Height A – Height C**		
Silt	**Height C – Height B**		

3 Use this chart to decide the sort of soil you have:

	Soil Sample 1	Soil sample 2
Clay soil: Half or more is clay		
Loam soil: Mostly silt and sand		
Sandy soil: Mostly sand		

4 Repeat the experiment with a different soil sample and record your results.

___

___

___

___

16 Touch-typing soil

How can we classify soils by touching them?

Out in the paddock, farmers often assess soil texture by touching a soil sample with their fingers. The way the sample feels, stretches and forms a ball will determine its soil type.

What you need

soil samples

water

1 Collect a ¼ cup of soil.

2 Add a little water and knead the soil until it feels like playdough.

3 Roll the soil into a small ball. Does it stay together? Check the chart.

4 Gently squeeze the soil between your thumb and forefinger to make a ribbon of soil. Check the chart.

TARGETING STEM JOURNAL 4 @ PASCAL PRESS ISBN 9781925726091

Soil Classification Flowchart

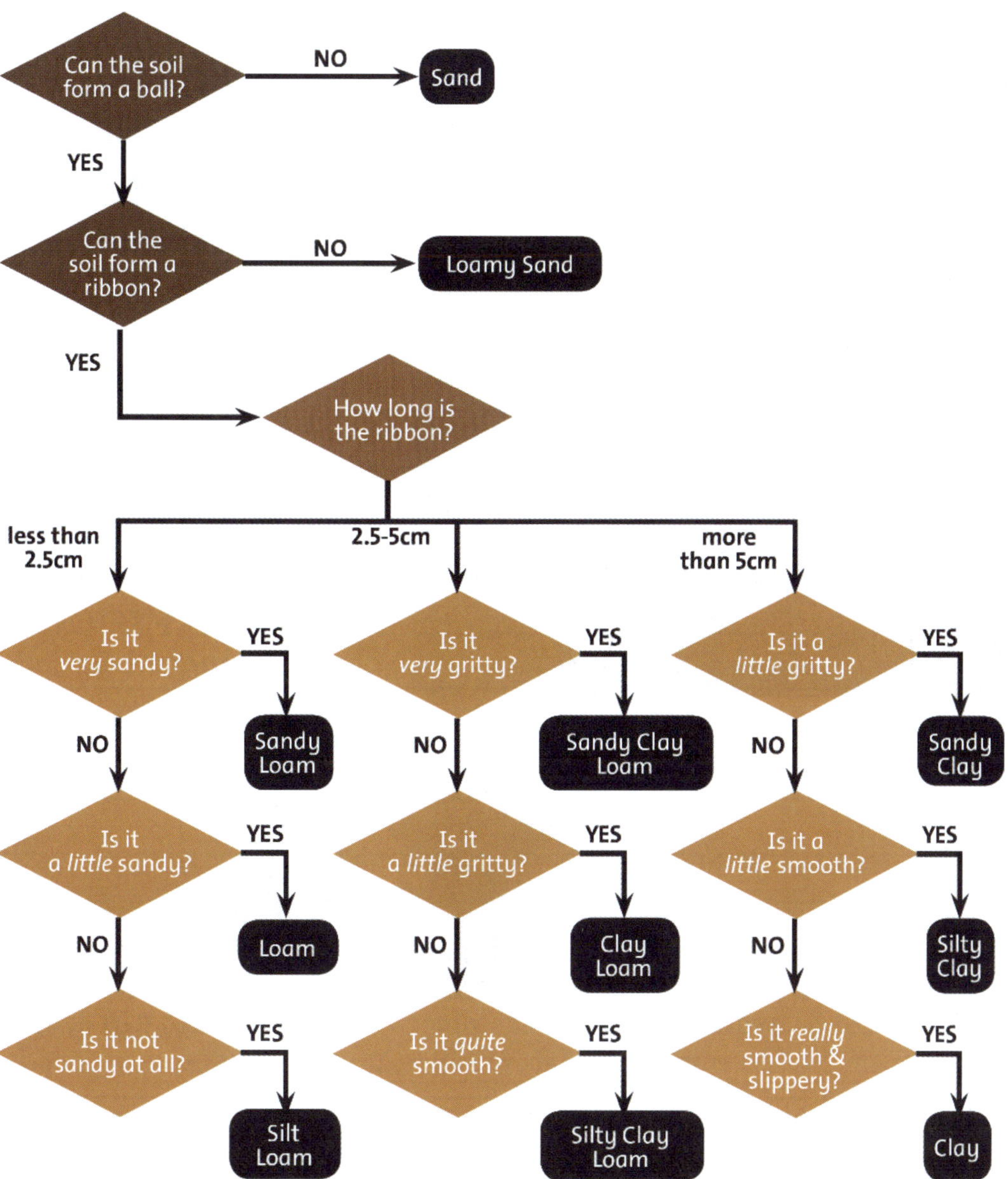

1 Check the two soil samples from Unit 15. How do the results compare? What does this tell you about the two different systems?

Classification	Soil Sample 1	Soil sample 2
Unit 15 Classification		
Unit 16 Classification		

2 As a class, find, classify and display as many different types of soil as you can. What is the most common soil in your local area? Which soils were you unable to find?

____

____

____

Soil erosion

How can we reduce soil erosion?

Soil erosion occurs when soil is moved from one place to another. This can happen naturally by the wind, running water or glaciers. It can also be caused by humans through farming, land clearing and climate change.

What you need

two large plastic bottles

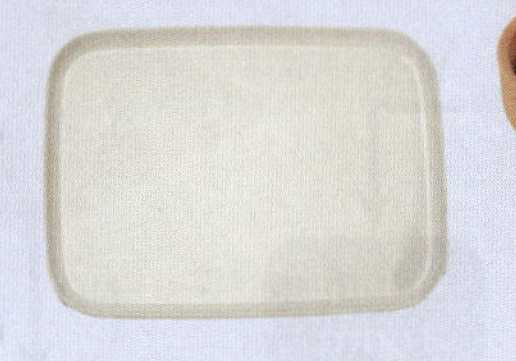
four cups

waterproof tray

container of soil

gravel, small rocks, sand

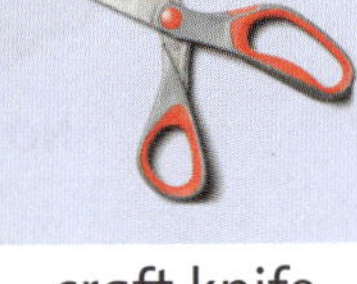
craft knife or scissors

1 Carefully cut the bottles in half, long way.

2 Arrange the four halves along the edge of the tray.

3 Add soil to each bottle. Add the gravel, rocks and plants as shown.

4 Pour in 200ml of water. Collect the run-off in the cups.

SCIENCE SSU074, SSU075, SIS065, SIS068, SIS071

MATHEMATICS MMG084, MMG290, MMG090

TARGETING STEM JOURNAL 4 @ PASCAL PRESS ISBN 9781925726091

1 Wait for 10 minutes. Water and sediment (run-off soil) will collect in the cups.

a. Strain out the water from each cup into a measuring container. Record the volume of water on the chart.

b. Weigh and record the mass of the cup and remaining sediment.

c. Weigh an empty cup. Calculate the mass of the water and sediment.

Container	Soil	Soil and sand	Soil and gravel	Soil and rocks
Volume of water				
Mass of cup and sediment				
Mass of sediment				

2 Graph your results on the chart below.

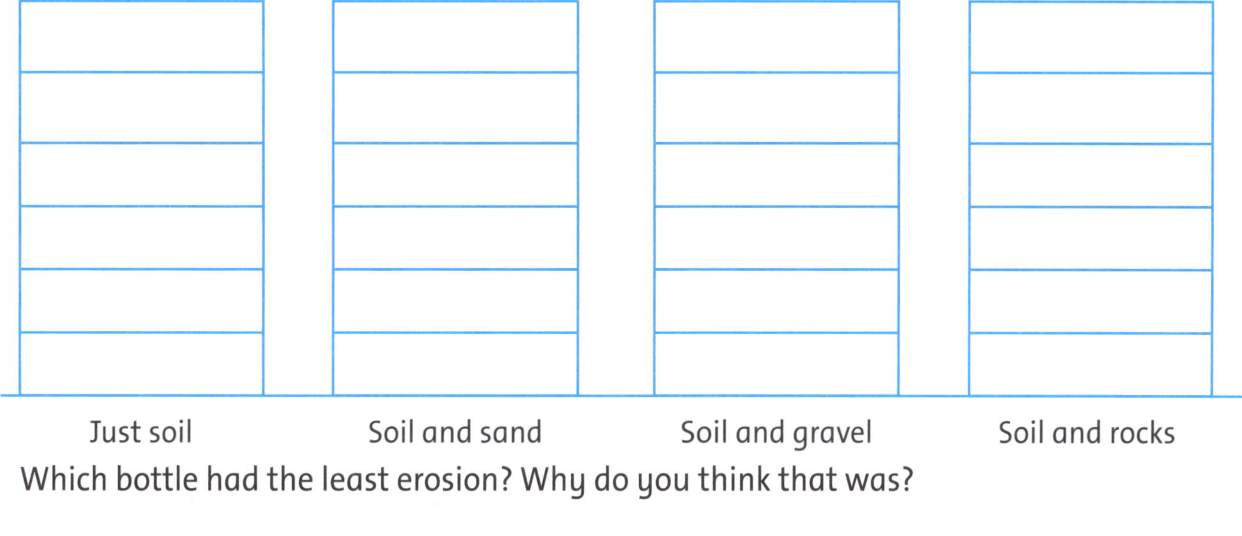

Which bottle had the least erosion? Why do you think that was?

____

____

____

3 Would having plants in the soil reduce soil erosion? Would building terraces reduce erosion? Devise an experiment to test both.

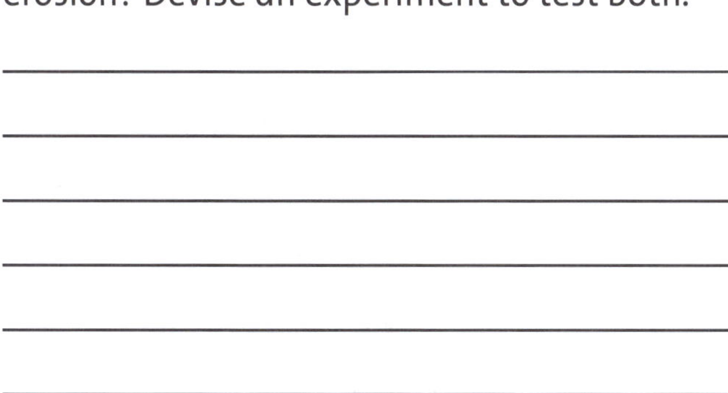

CHALLENGE

Soil profiles

How can we make a soil profile?

The different layers of soil in the photograph are called soil horizons. The soil in each horizon differs in colour, texture and size. The way these horizons are arranged is called a soil profile.

What you need

a pit or cutting

A4 cardboard

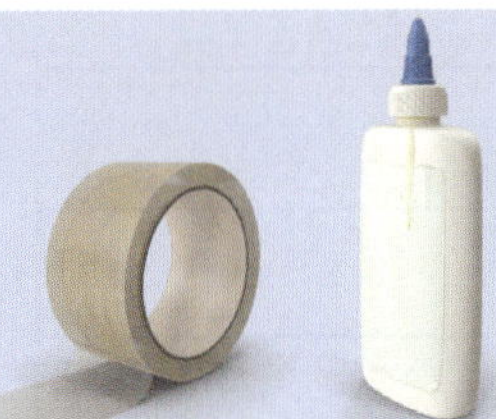

glue or double sided-sticky tape

tape measure

1 Cut the cardboard into four 5cm-wide strips.

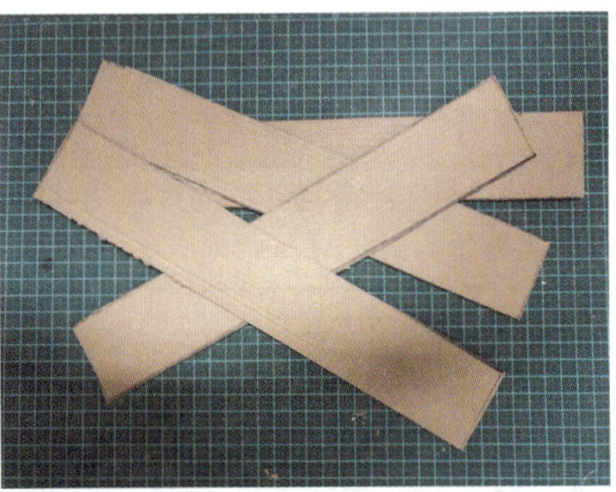

2 Glue the strips together. Rule a scale down the side, marking every 20cm up to 120cm.

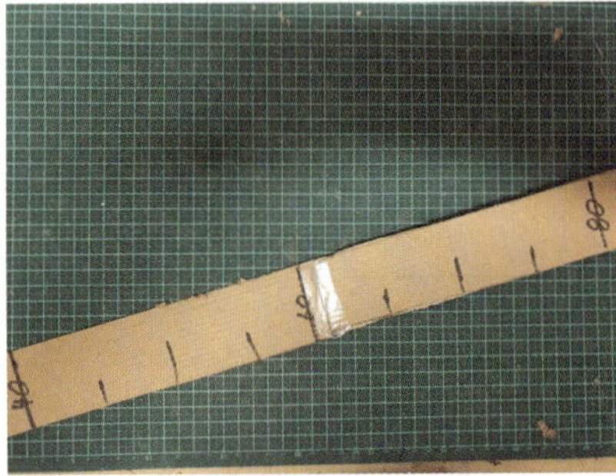

3 Measure the depth of each horizon and mark it on the profile.

4 Glue samples from each horizon onto the profile.

1 Most soil profiles have three horizons.

Horizon A	Horizon B	Horizon C
Surface (topsoil)	Subsoil	Substratum
Roots, earthworms	Some roots	
Humus	Small stones	Larger stones

- Label this soil profile with Horizon A, Horizon B and Horizon C.
- The rock layer at the bottom isn't soil. Label it Horizon R.
- Label your soil profile with the same headings.

2 It isn't practical to make and store full scale versions of soil profiles. Instead, scaled-down versions are used. Make a scaled-down version of soil profile that will fit on a single sheet of A4 paper. It will be ¼ the size.

a. Calculate the measurements below:

Full Scale	20cm	40cm	60cm	80cm	100cm	120cm
¼ scale	20/4=5	40/4=				

b. Rule a line down the centre of the card.

c. Use the chart to add the scale marks. Label them with the full-scale measurements.

d. Measure the depth of each horizon on the original profile. Draw the horizons onto the scaled-down version.

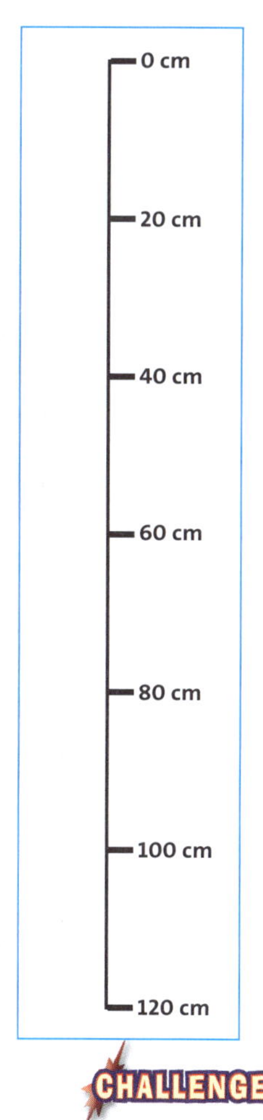

WHAT ARE SOIL PROFILES USED FOR?

Measuring the fertility of soil is important for growing crops. Soil profiles show if layers have high or low amounts of organic material and if nutrients are staying in the soil.

Drain away!

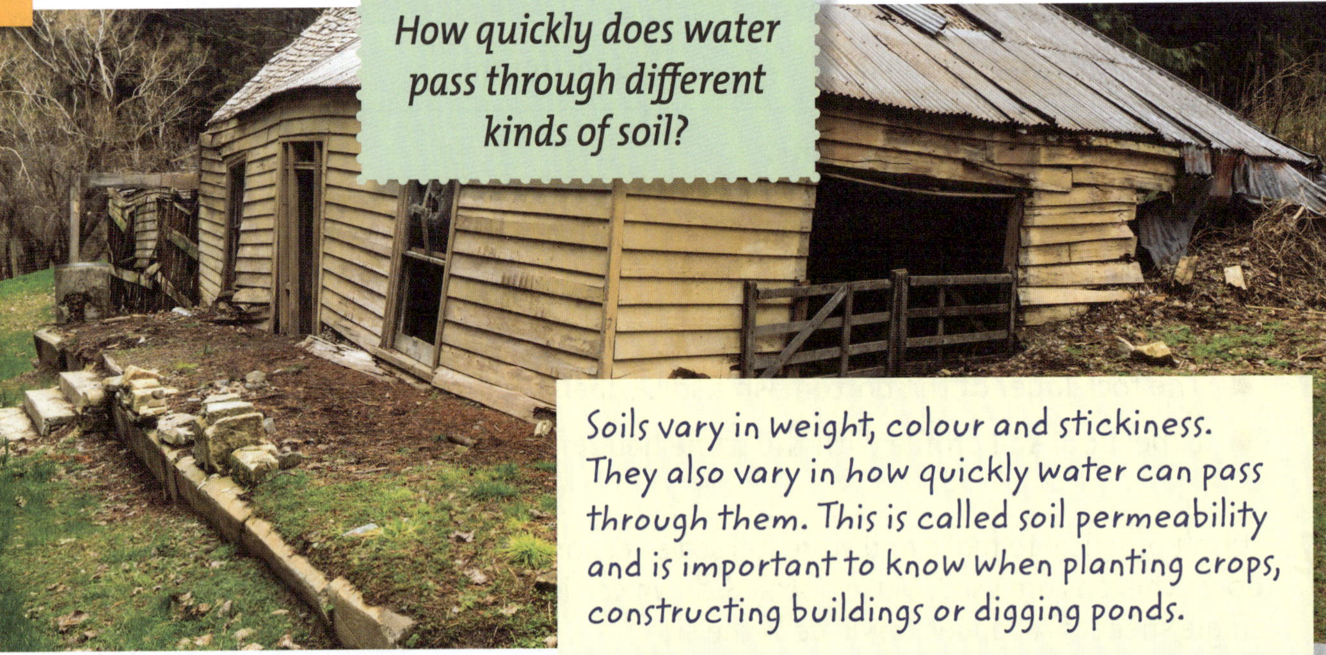

How quickly does water pass through different kinds of soil?

Soils vary in weight, colour and stickiness. They also vary in how quickly water can pass through them. This is called soil permeability and is important to know when planting crops, constructing buildings or digging ponds.

What you need

8 paper cups

four different kinds of soil

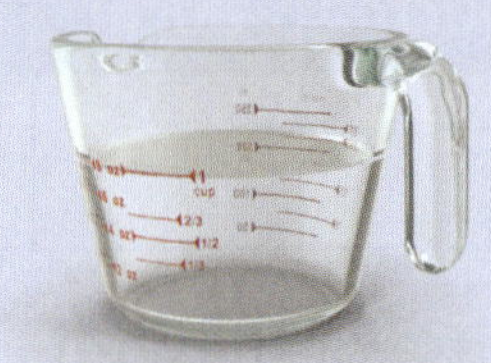

measuring flask

thick card

cotton wool

1 Punch a hole in the bottom of cups 1-4. These are the soil cups.

2 Cut out four squares of card larger than the opening of the cups. Cut a hole the size of a twenty cent coin in their centres.

3 Place the card squares on top of cups 5-8. These are the drainage cups. Balance the 4 soil cups on top.

4 Fill the soil cups with 100g of the four different kinds of soil. Place cotton wool in the top.

TARGETING STEM JOURNAL 4 @ PASCAL PRESS ISBN 9781925726091

1 Look at the soils and predict which one will be the most permeable (allows the most water to run through it).

I predict that ______________________ will be the most permeable because

____.

Slowly pour 100ml of water into each of the soil cups. Wait five minutes then measure the volume of water in the drainage cups.

	Soil 1	Soil 2	Soil 3	Soil 4
Volume of drainage water (ml)				

Was your prediction correct? Explain your results.

____

____

2 Predict what would happen if you poured another 100ml of water into the now damp soils.

I predict that the same / more / less amount of water will pass through because

____.

Empty the drainage cups and reposition them below the soil cups. Slowly pour 100ml into each soil cup. Wait five minutes then measure the volume of water in the drainage cups.

	Soil 1	Soil 2	Soil 3	Soil 4
Volume of drainage water (ml)				

3 Graph the volume of drainage for each soil for the two experiments.

	Soil 1 Dry	Soil 1 Wet	Soil 2 Dry	Soil 2 Wet	Soil 3 Dry	Soil 3 Wet	Soil 4 Dry	Soil 4 Wet
90								
80								
70								
60								
50								
40								
30								
20								
10								

4 Which soil would be best for the bottom of a fish pond? Explain your answer.

____

____

Worm farming

What you need

a small aquarium or similar transparent container

different types of soil

dead leaves

30-40 earthworms

1 Add the soil in layers. Try not to mix the layers.

2 Cover the top layer of soil with the dead leaves.

3 Add the earthworms.

4 Cover the top.

1 Keep a Journal over a month. Include **Changes observed** such as tunnels, earthworm casts, leaves eaten or the mixing of soil levels. Record any **Maintenance** you do, such as adding water to keep the soil damp, adding more leaves or removing food that the worms aren't eating.

Day / date	Changes observed	Maintenance

2 Which of the changes that you observed would be helpful to plants? Explain your answer below.

____

____

____

3 Make a stop animation of the changes.

a. Make a stand to support your camera or tablet.

b. Take a photo at the beginning and end of each day.

c. Assemble the photos into a video.

BIOTURBATION

Bioturbation is the process by which soil is worked over by animals and plants. Animals such as earthworms are called bioturbators and classified as ecosystem engineers.

BUYING WORMS

Worms can be bought online and delivered by courier. As a guide, 1000 worms cost about $50, or about 5c each.

Rubber band tester

SCIENCE SSU074, SSU076, SHE061, SIS065, SIS068, SIS071

MATHEMATICS MMG084, MMG090, MSP095, MSP096

How can we measure the strength of a rubber band?

When you stretch a rubber band, you store energy in it. When you let go, that stored energy changes to moving energy which can exert a force on objects touching it.

What you need

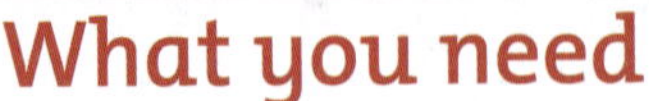

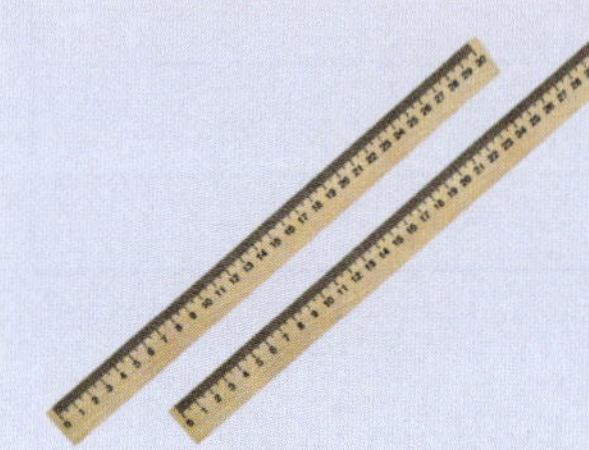

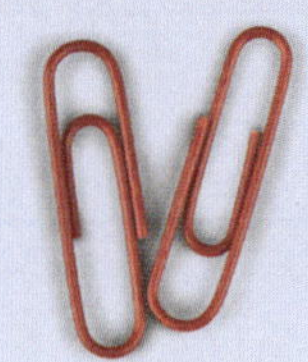

2 wooden rulers | 4 rubber bands | 2 paperclips | a wood or plastic block | stack of coins or washers

1 Bind the two rulers together with a rubber band at the 30cm end.

2 Place the block in between them in the centre. Wrap a rubber band on either side.

3 Slide the paperclips onto the 4th rubber band.

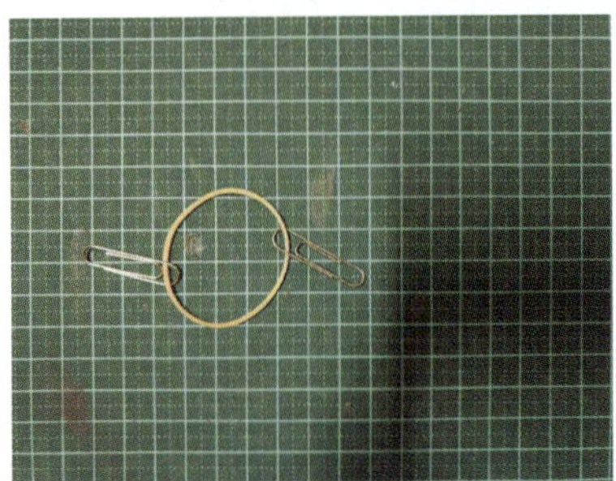

4 Push the paperclips onto the ends of the ruler.

TARGETING STEM JOURNAL 4 @ PASCAL PRESS ISBN 9781925726091

1 Test the launcher with a taped-together stack of coins or washers.

- a Find a smooth surface, such as a floor, and place the launcher on it.
- b Pull back the rubber band to the 10cm mark.
- c Place the stack of coins in the launcher and release the rubber band. Record the distance the stack travels.

Rubber band stretch	10cm	9cm	8cm	7cm	6cm	5cm	4cm	3cm	2cm	1cm
Predicted distance										
Travel distance										

- d Predict how far the stack will travel for the other distances.
- e Repeat steps b and c for the other distances. How accurate were your predictions?

____

____

____

- f Graph your results.

Distance the coins travel (cm)

80										
70										
60										
50										
40										
30										
20										
10										
	10	9	8	7	6	5	4	3	2	1

Rubber band stretch (cm)

TAKING IT FURTHER

Predict, then test, the effect of :

- Thicker / thinner / shorter / longer / more rubber bands
- More / less coins
- A toy car instead of a stack of coins
- Other surfaces such as carpet, stone or plastic

Use the launcher carefully and only on the ground. Do not aim it at other people or at fragile objects.

TARGETING STEM JOURNAL 4 @ PASCAL PRESS ISBN 9781925726091

Magnetic boats

Magnets can exert a force on metals containing iron, such as steel. This force can act from a distance without the two objects touching. It can also act through non-magnetic materials, such as plastics.

How can we make a boat move on water using a magnet?

What you need

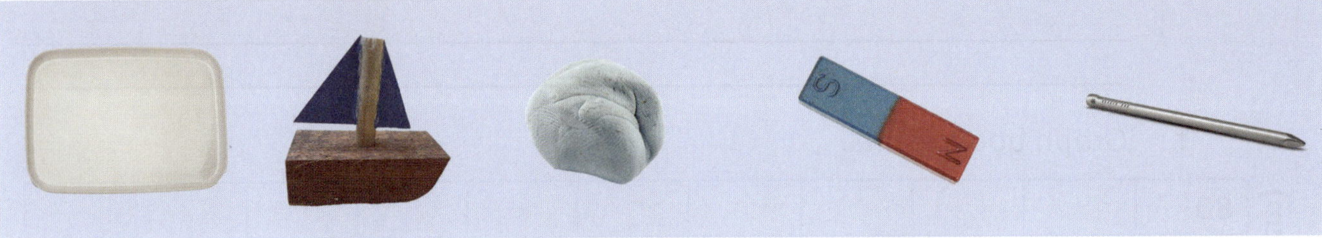

large, waterproof plastic tray

small toy boat

mounting putty (such as Blu-Tack)

strong magnet (NOT neodymium)

large nail, screw or flat steel

1 Attach the washers onto the boat's hull.

2 Attach the magnet to the pencil or dowel.

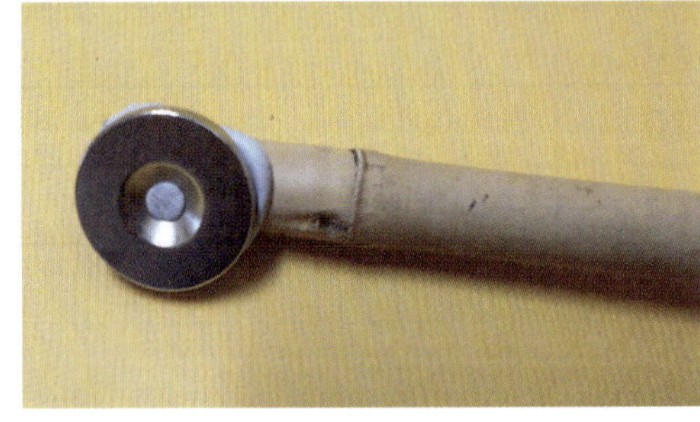

3 Support the tray on blocks and fill it with water.

4 Use the magnet below the tray to move the boat on the water.

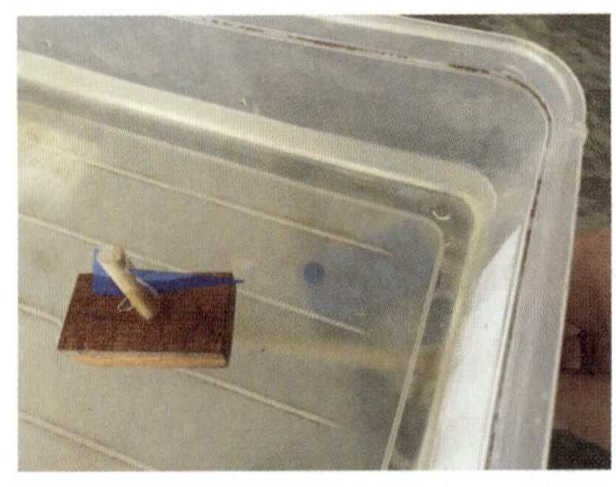

TARGETING STEM JOURNAL 4 @ PASCAL PRESS ISBN 9781925726091

1 Add more water to the tray. What's the greatest depth you can have before the magnet won't work on the boat?

Depth of water (cm)	Does the magnet move the boat?	Observations

2 What effect does adding more metal under the boat have?

____

____

____

3 Design a water maze for the boat to go through. Will the maze float on the surface or sit on the bottom of the tray? Could you include magnetic objects in the maze? Draw your design below, then test it out.

Neodymium rare earth magnets are very strong and can pose a health danger if swallowed. In 2013, Australia banned the sale of magnets which were small, very strong and sold as part of games, construction kits or jewellery.

TARGETING STEM JOURNAL 4 @ PASCAL PRESS ISBN 9781925726091

Salt and pepper electrostatics

How can we separate salt and pepper using static electricity?

Rubbing plastic objects can build up a static charge on them. Like magnets, objects with the same charge will repel and objects with the opposite charge will attract.

What you need

salt and pepper

plastic comb

cardboard

1 Shake salt onto the cardboard.

2 Shake pepper over the top.

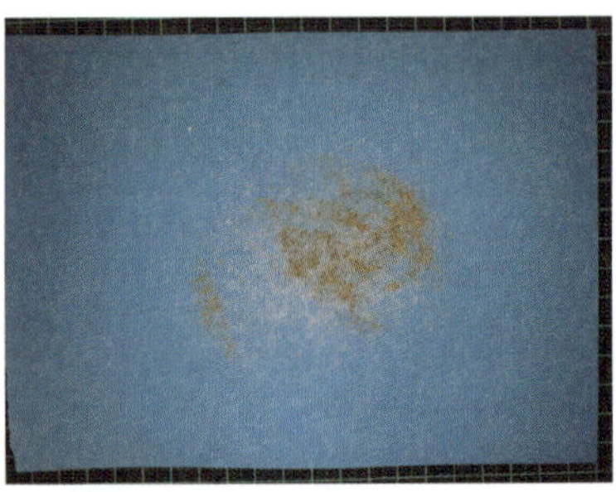

3 Rub the comb on wool material or through your hair to build up an electrostatic charge.

4 Bring the comb towards the salt and pepper.

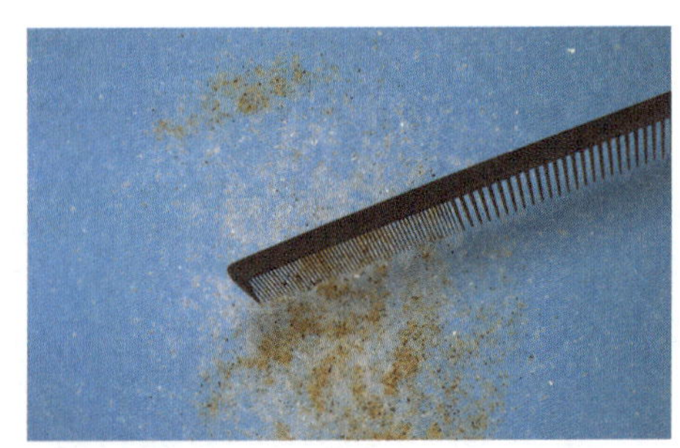

TARGETING STEM JOURNAL 4 @ PASCAL PRESS ISBN 9781925726091

1 How close did the comb have to be to attract the pepper? What happens if you get closer? Can you make the salt jump onto the comb? Why do you think the pepper 'jumped' first?

2 The pepper was attracted to the comb because it had a different charge. What if two objects have the same charge? Rub a plastic ruler on wool then balance it on top of a bottle. Rub a second plastic ruler and hold the end near the first ruler. What happens? Can you explain why?

3 Static electricity can damage electronic equipment so technicians often wear a static-discharge cable. Rub a comb through your hair to make it stand up. What objects can you touch in the classroom to get rid of your static hair? List them below.

4 A factory has a tall chimney. People in its neighbourhood are complaining about the smoke particles landing on their houses, gardens and washing. Design a machine to attract the smoke particles before they leave the chimney. How will you charge the collecting 'comb'? How will you remove the particles when the 'comb' is full?

Electromagnet

How can we make a magnet you can turn on and off?

An electromagnet is only magnetic when it has electricity flowing through its coils. Like normal magnets, electromagnets only attract metals with iron in them.

What you need

D-size battery

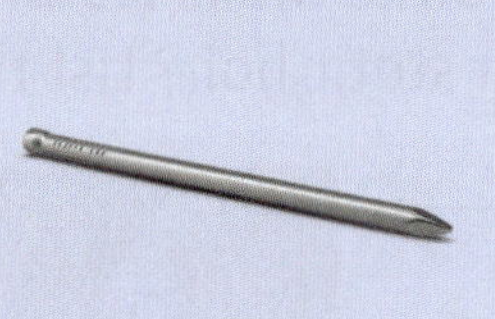
large iron nail

1m of coated copper wire

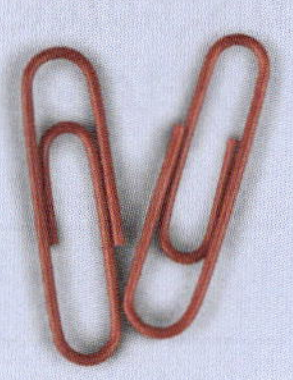
paperclips

1 Cut the coating away from the ends of the wire.

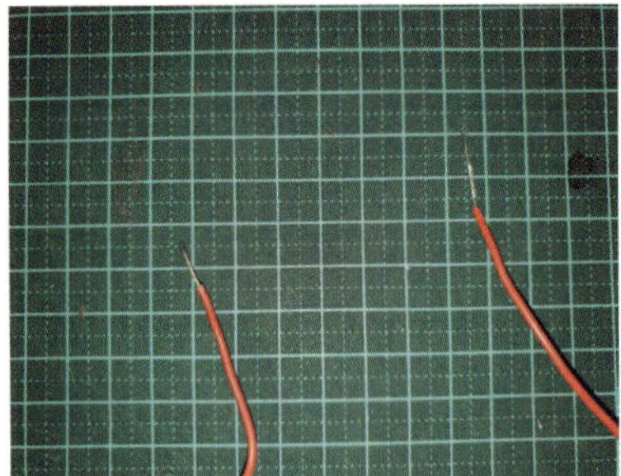

2 Starting 20cm along, wrap the wire around the nail. Take care not to overlap. Leave 20cm at the other end.

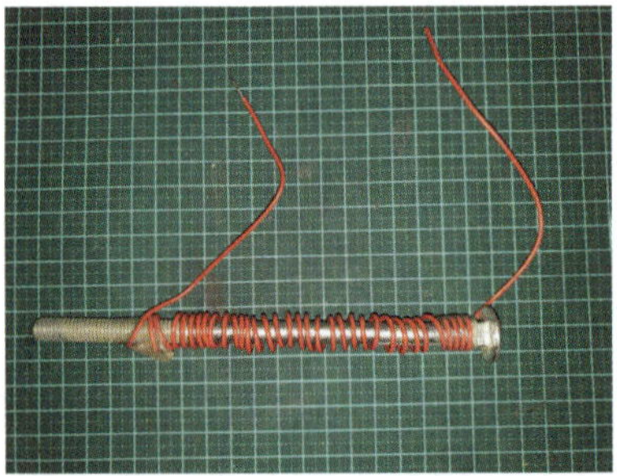

3 Tape one end to the bottom of the battery.

4 Touch the other end to the top of the battery and hold the nail near some paperclips.

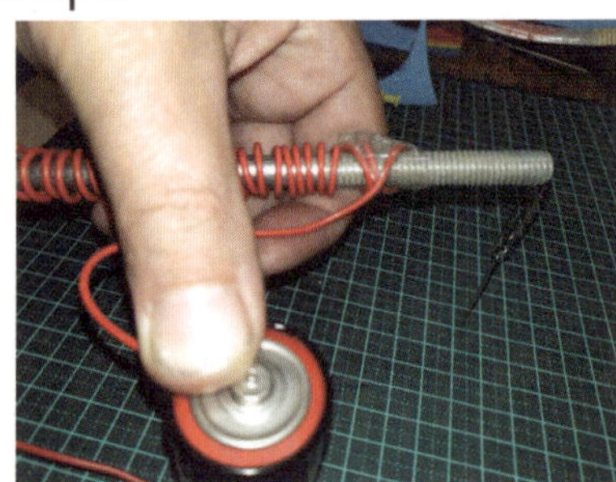

TARGETING STEM JOURNAL 4 @ PASCAL PRESS ISBN 9781925726091

1 Test the electromagnet:

  a From how far away will it pick up a paperclip?
  b What happens if you unwrap some of the wire?
  c What difference do you think a thicker or longer *nail* will make?
  d What difference do you think a thicker *wire* will make?

2 List the advantages and disadvantages of using an electromagnet in a junkyard.

Advantages	Disadvantages

3 Oh, no! The evil villain Electromagneto is on the loose! And it's not his good looks that are attracting attention! Experiment with your electromagnet to discover what Electromagneto *can't* magnetise through. Plan your experiment below, then test different materials such as wood, plastic, water, aluminium, steel and glass.

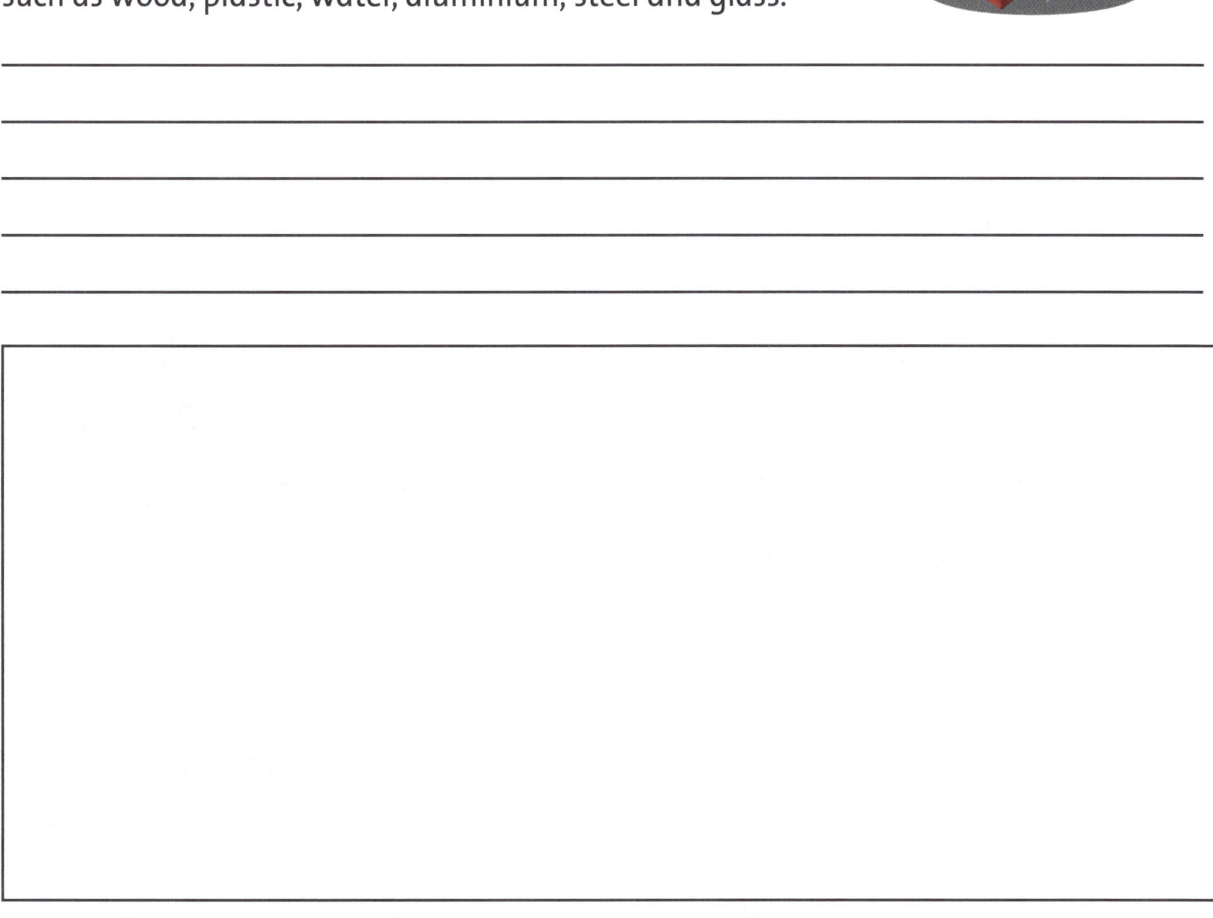

The battery can become quite warm with repeated use. Disconnect the wires when you are not experimenting.

TARGETING STEM JOURNAL 4 @ PASCAL PRESS ISBN 9781925726091

Bubble shapes

Can we make bubbles in different shapes?

The air inside, the air outside and a force called surface tension pulls a bubble into its almost spherical shape. Bubbles moving through a liquid, such as air bubbles through water, can be flattened at the top.

SCIENCE SSU076, SHE061, SIS065, SIS068, SIS071

MATHEMATICS MMG088

What you need

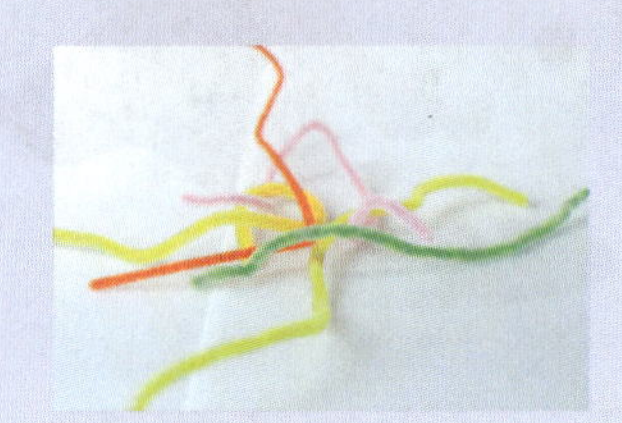
pipe cleaners

bubble mixture

waterproof container

1 Make bubble mixture from the recipe on the next page.

2 Form the pipe cleaners into different shape 'wands' such as squares, triangles or stars.

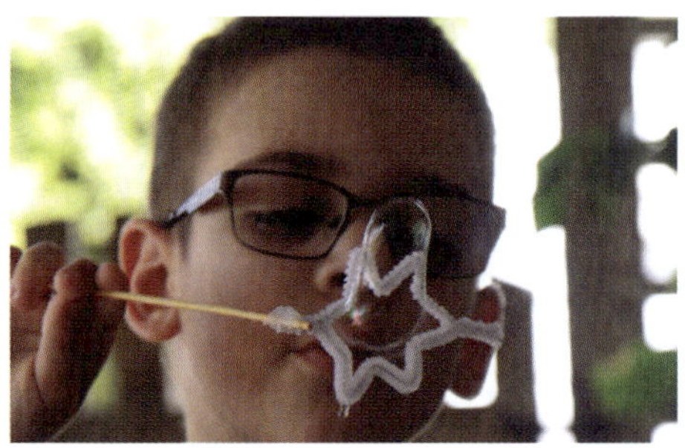

3 'Blow' bubbles through your designs.

4 Record the shapes you create on the Journal chart.

TARGETING STEM JOURNAL 4 @ PASCAL PRESS ISBN 9781925726091

1 What shapes were the bubbles formed by the different bubble wands?

Wand Shape	Square	Triangle		
Bubble Shape Formed				
Observations				

2 Try making a 3D cube wand.

- **a** Bend a pipe cleaner into a cube.
- **b** Dip the cube-wand into the mixture. Lift the wand and shake it from side to side.

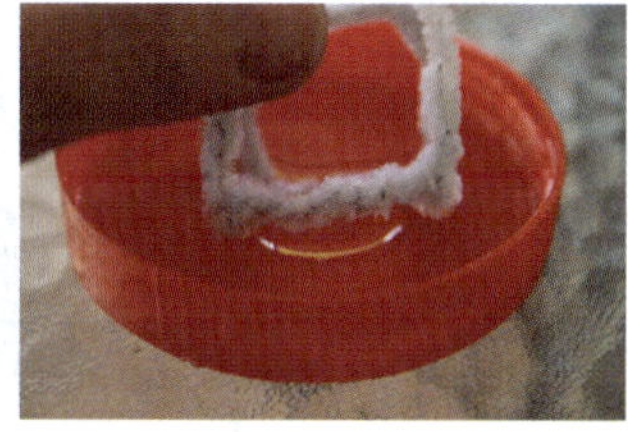

- **c** Draw the shape you see below:

3 Experiment with other 3D shapes such as a triangular prism, a square-based pyramid or a cone. Draw the bubbles they create below.

BUBBLE MIXTURE RECIPE

Ingredients:

- 350ml water
- 150ml detergent
- 25ml glycerine

Stir the ingredients together. If possible, leave overnight.

TARGETING STEM JOURNAL 4 @ PASCAL PRESS ISBN 9781925726091

Cam-powered automata

How can we use cams to make a moving toy?

A camshaft is a cylindrical shaft with cams attached to it. In a car, the camshaft rotation opens and closes the valves that let fuel and air into the engine and exhaust gases out.

What you need

corrugated cardboard

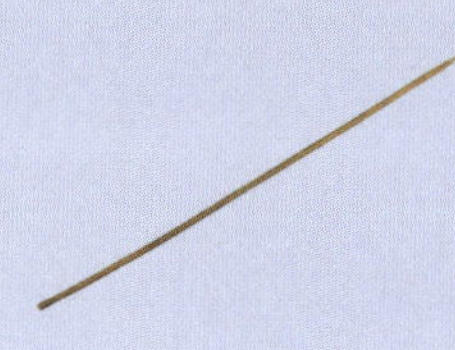

skewers

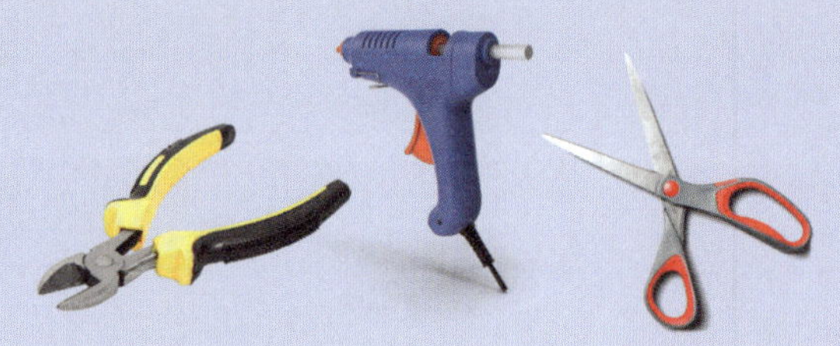

side cutters, hot glue gun, scissors

1 Build the frame from corrugated cardboard.

2 Cut out a cam using the pattern as a guide. Glue a 15cm strip of card around its edge.

3 Cut the end off a skewer. Carefully push it through one end of the frame.

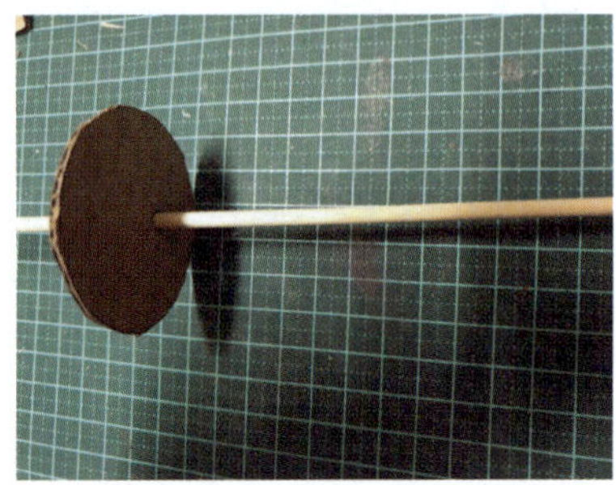

4 Push the skewer through the centre of the cam. Glue in place. This is the camshaft.

TARGETING STEM JOURNAL 4 @ PASCAL PRESS ISBN 9781925726091

5 Push the skewer out the other side of the frame. Cut the sharp end off. 	**6** Push a skewer through vertically from the top, above the cam. 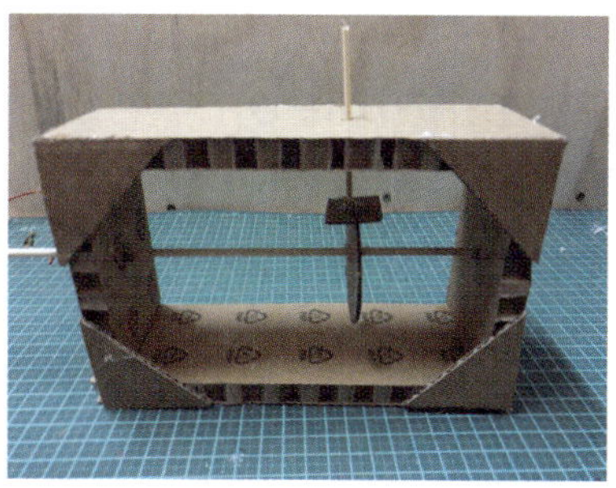
7 Cut the sharp ends off. Glue a small card foot to the bottom. 	**8** Rotate the camshaft. The vertical skewer should move up and down. 

1 Add a second cam to the camshaft. Glue it in place at a different angle to the first. Add a second vertical skewer above the second cam.

2 Make cardboard figures to attach to the skewers. Consider having a theme such as 'In the Jungle', 'Under the Sea' or 'Haunted House'.

3 Add scenery and props. You could add a bush that a cam-creature hides behind or a trapdoor that a cam-monster emerges from.

CAMSHAFT CHALLENGES

- Add a handle to the camshaft to make turning easier.
- Design a creature that has a cam-operated leg or arm, with the rest of the creature staying still.
- Design a flapping bird or insect, whose wings are operated by moving skewers.

Marble ramp

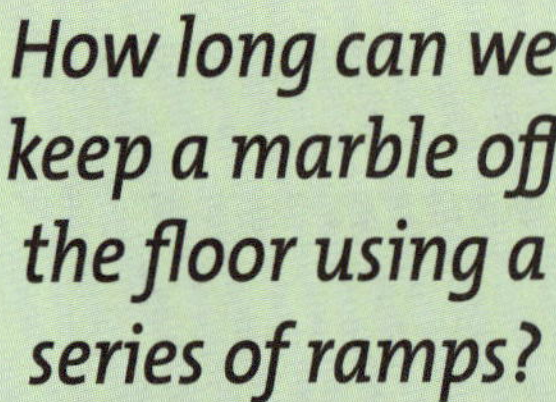

How long can we keep a marble off the floor using a series of ramps?

Ramps are a type of simple machine called inclined plane. Look at the ramp in the photograph. The ramp's gentle slope allows wheelchairs and prams easier access to the beach.

What you need

large sheet of thick corrugated cardboard	cardboard tubes	pins	marbles	scissors

1 Cut the tubes in half, lengthwise.

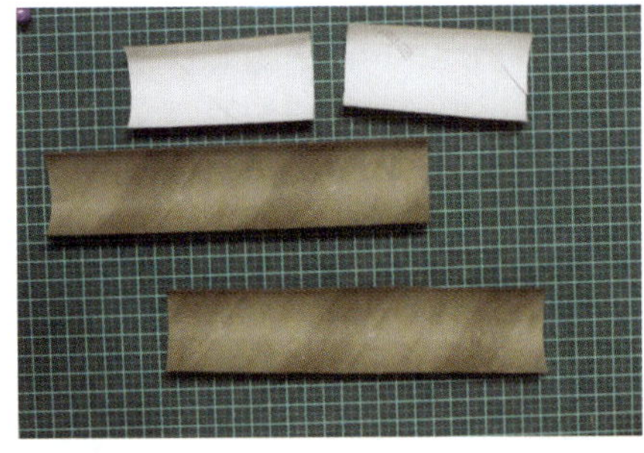

2 Lean the corrugated cardboard against a wall.

3 Pin the half-tubes onto the board so that a marble can roll from one to another.

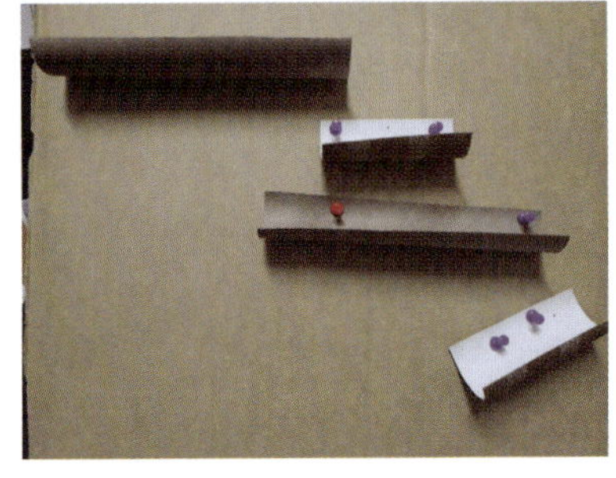

4 Time the marble rolling from the top to the bottom.

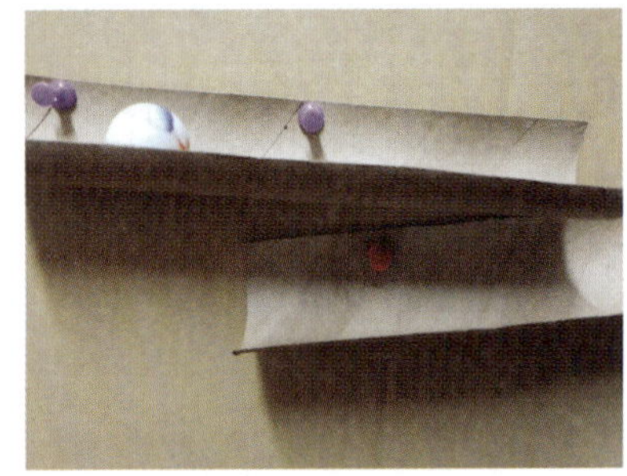

SCIENCE SSU074, SSU076, SIS065

MATHEMATICS MMG084, MSP095, MSP096

1 Run the marble down the ramp four times as you time it. Record the results below. What could you adjust to make the run slower? Make the changes and run the marble again.

Run No.	Time (secs)
1	
2	
3	
4	

Run No.	Time (secs)
1	
2	
3	
4	

2 Calculate the **total length of half-tubes** used for your marble ramp. Divide this total by your best marble-ramp time. This is your marble's average speed in centimetres per second.

Total length of half-tubes (cm) / Best time (seconds) = ______ cm/s

How does this compare to other students? Who has the best (slowest!) speed?

______

______

______

3 How else could you slow the marble down without actually stopping it? Consider how you could use: sponge, pins, cloth, corrugated cardboard, tissues, plasticine, glue, aluminium foil. Read the box on 'traffic calming'. Can you use any of those techniques? Sketch out some ideas below.

TRAFFIC CALMING

Engineers use 'traffic calming' techniques to slow traffic. These techniques include:

- Speed humps and speed tables (wider humps)
- Rumble strips (closely spaced raised strips)
- Chicanes (narrowing of the road)

Rubber band powered boat

How can we propel a boat using rubber band power?

Paddleboats are propelled by a motor turning a series of paddles at the sides or stern of the boat. The paddles push water backward and the boat forward.

What you need

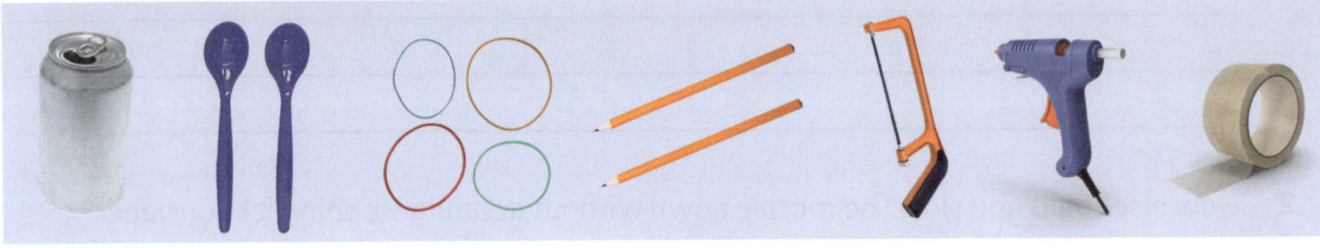

empty drink can | 2 plastic teaspoons | rubber bands | old pencils or canes | saw | glue gun | tape

1 Cut two 20cm lengths of cane. Attach them firmly to either side of the can.

2 Cut the handles of the two spoons. Join them together, scoops facing in opposite directions.

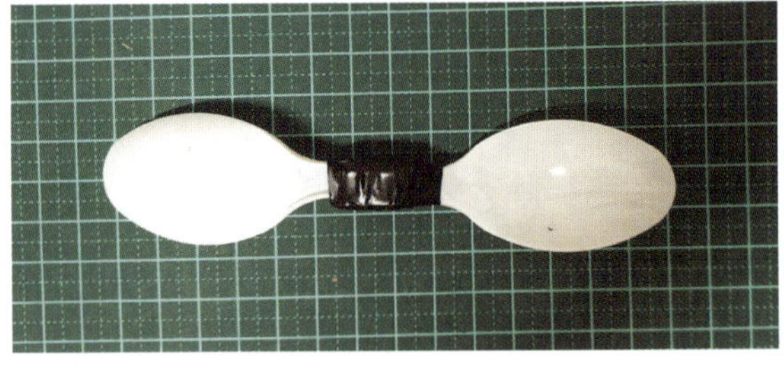

3 Thread a rubber band around the ends of the canes.

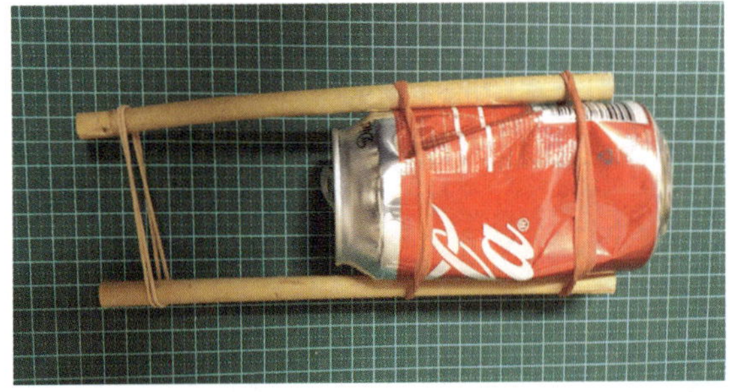

4 Push the spoons through the rubber band. Place the boat in water, wind up and release.

TARGETING STEM JOURNAL 4 @ PASCAL PRESS ISBN 9781925726091

1 Test your paddleboat in a tray of water.

What went well	What didn't go well	How I could fix it

2 The Murray River Rubber Band Paddleboat competition is coming soon with a huge prize for the paddleboat that travels the furthest on its rubber band power. Before you try improving your paddleboat's sailing range, record its current statistics (model 1).

	Mass (g)	Length (cm)	Maximum travel distance (cm)	Engine size (no. of rubber bands)	Paddle type
Model 1				1	Spoons x 2
Model 2					
Model 3					
Model 4					

3 Choose one or more of the ideas below to improve your boat's sailing range. Sketch out a new design, then test and record the results above.

- **a** Increase the number of rubber bands.
- **b** Increase the number of paddles. You may need to use a different system than spoons. Consider using a cork and plastic fins.
- **c** The can is quite light and may not stay in the water. Add some ballast by pouring water into it.
- **d** The bow (front) of your paddleboat is flat. Consider making it more streamlined, so it moves more easily through the water.
- **e** Many boats have a keel to keep them upright. Consider adding a plastic one underneath the can.

Galton marble run

How can we test how randomly marbles fall?

Sir Francis Galton invented the 'Galton Board' in 1860. Balls are dropped in the top and bounce randomly off rows of pins. Bins collect the balls at the bottom, making a 'graph' of their trip.

What you need

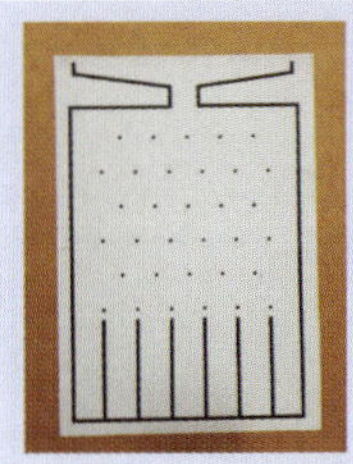

Galton Board template

36 coloured push pins

A4 corrugated card

marbles

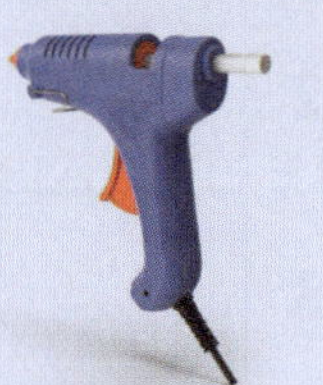

glue gun

glue stick

1 Photocopy the template on p 87 and paste onto the corrugated card.

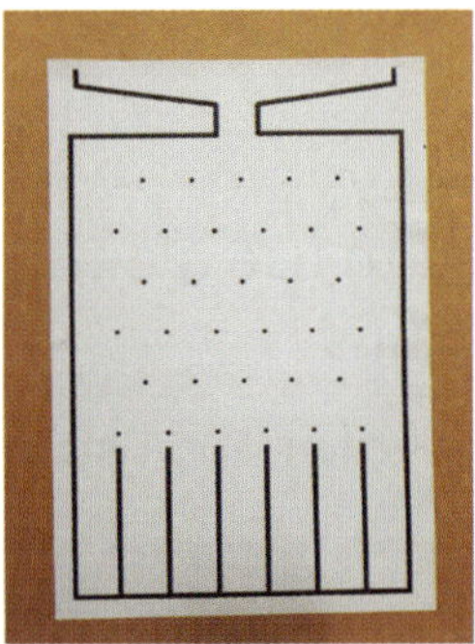

2 Press the push pins into each of the holes. Test to check the marbles run through smoothly.

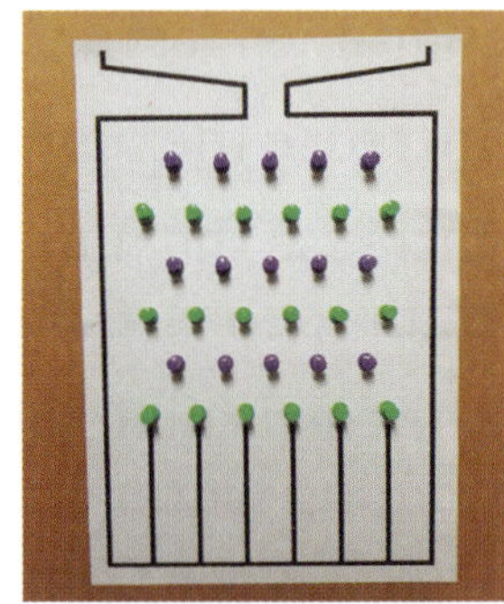

3 Cut 2cm strips from the card. Glue onto the black lines.

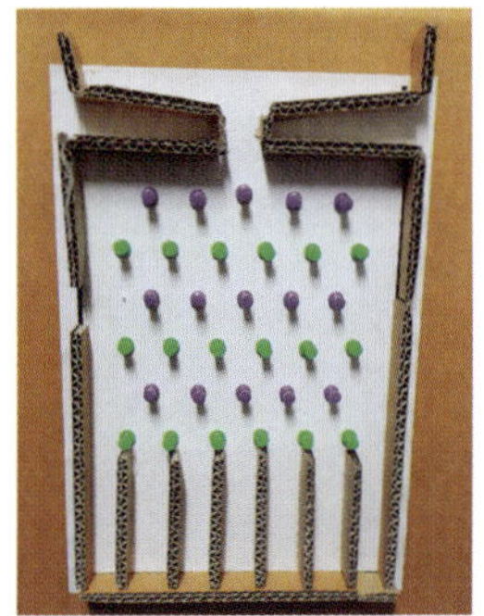

4 Glue a support on the back to create a slope.

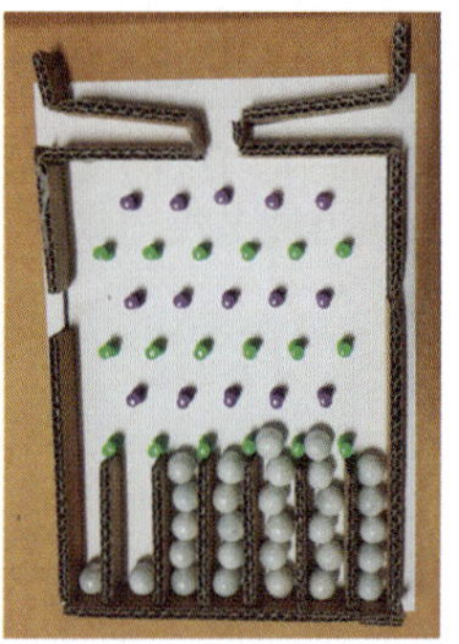

TARGETING STEM JOURNAL 4 @ PASCAL PRESS ISBN 9781925726091

1 Test your Galton Board by running single marbles down. Make notes below of any problems such as marbles jamming, falling off the board or not rolling. Adjust your board to fix the problems.

2 Experiment with the best way to release the marbles. Try loading all the marbles into the funnel, releasing them one by one or pouring them in from a container. Explain your choice.

3 Run 20 marbles through the board several times and record on the graphs below.

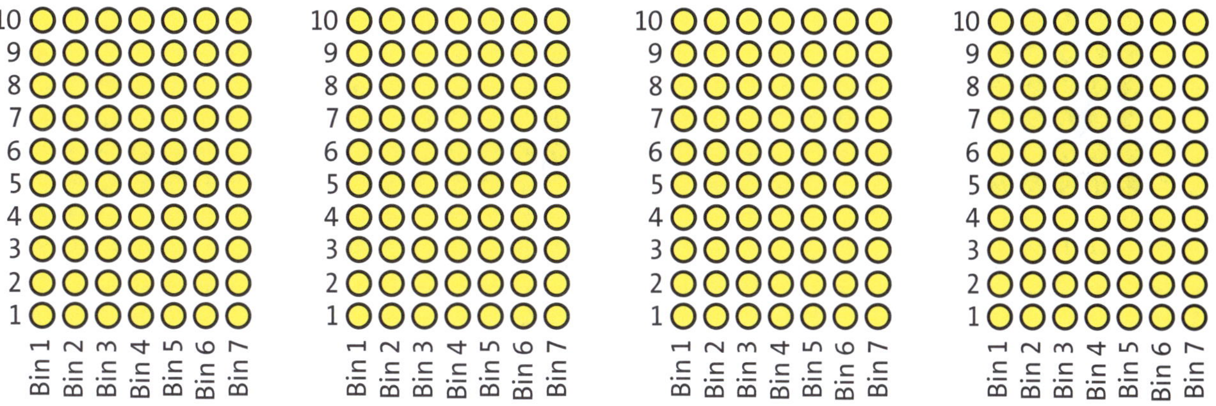

What do you notice? Which bins do the most balls fall in? Which bins have the least? Is there a pattern?

EXPANSION PACK

- Make a gate that releases the marbles in the 'funnel' at the top.
- Extend the collection bins for larger runs of marbles.

NOTES

- The template was designed for standard marbles that are 13-15mm in diameter.
- If you use a different size ball you will need to adjust the distance between the pins and the distance between the rows. This should be about 5mm more than the diameter of your ball.

Galton heads and tails

How can we model a Galton Board with coin tosses?

When a marble hits a peg on the Galton Board, it falls randomly either left or right. We can model this by using coins, which fall randomly 'heads' or 'tails'.

What you need

counters

coin

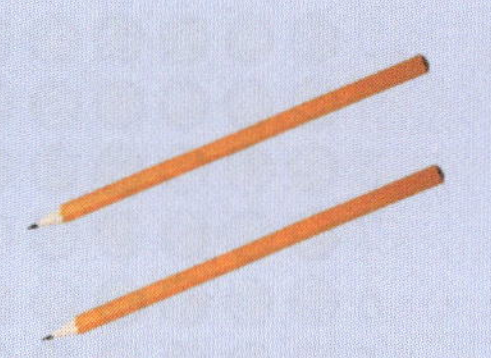
pencils

1 Place the counter at the top of the triangle.

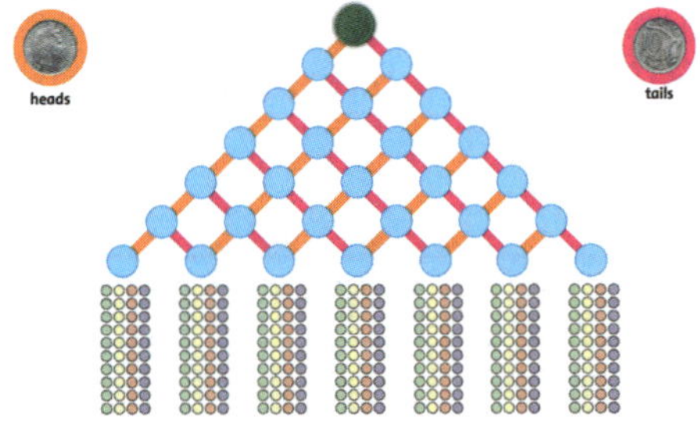

2 Toss the coin. If it lands 'heads', move down along the orange line. If it lands 'tails', move down along the magenta line.

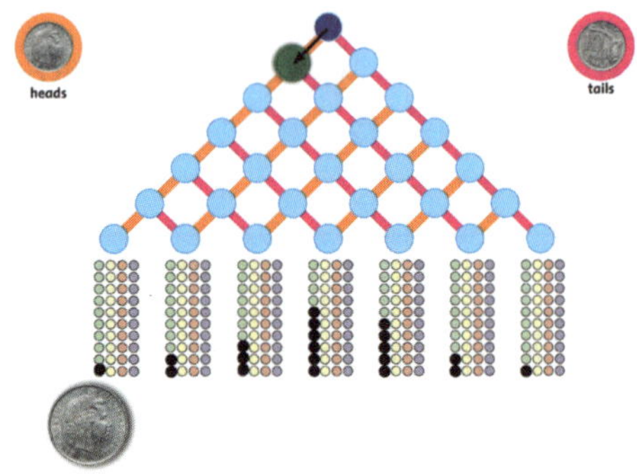

3 Repeat step 2 until you reach the bottom.

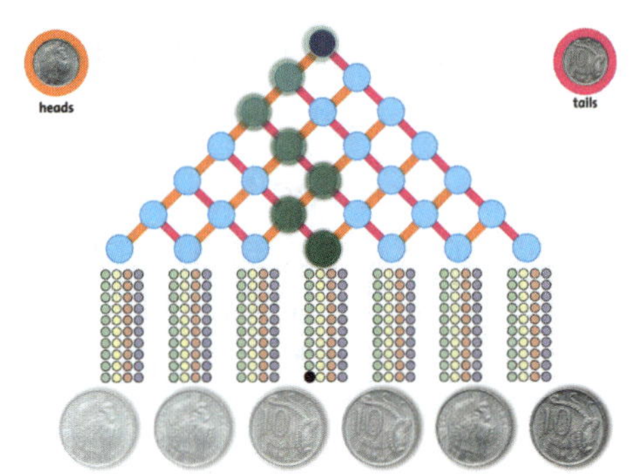

4 Colour a (green) circle to record the bin you ended on. Repeat for twenty runs through the board.

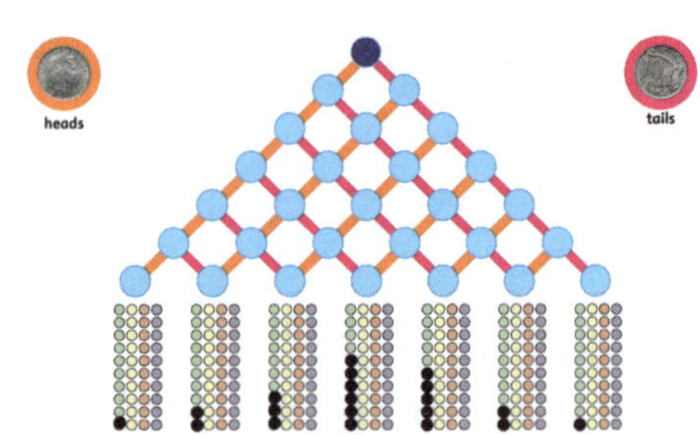

SCIENCE SSU076, SHE061, SIS065, SIS068, SIS071

MATHEMATICS MMG091, MSP092, MSP095, MSP096

TARGETING STEM JOURNAL 4 @ PASCAL PRESS ISBN 9781925726091

1 Record your run through the board on the green circle bins. How does the result compare to the board you made in Unit 28?

____

____

____

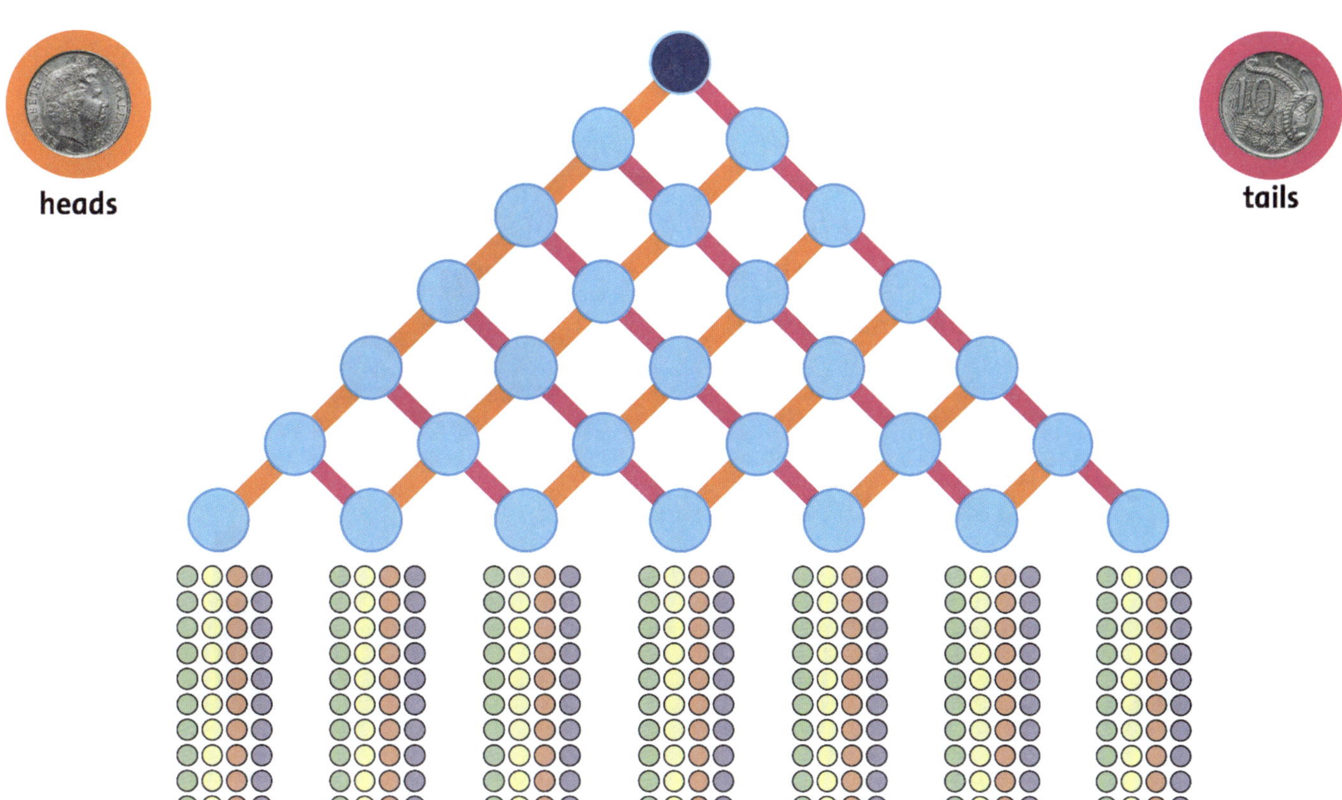

2 Play again, but this time, roll a dice. Move left (orange) for odd numbers (1, 3 and 5) and move right (magenta) for even numbers. Record in the yellow circle bins. Do you get a similar result?

3 Play again, but this time, roll the six dice at the same time. Record in the red circle bins.

4 Play again with dice but this time move left (orange) for the numbers 1 and 2 and right (magenta) for the numbers 3, 4, 5 and 6. What do you expect to happen?

____

____

____

Take a robot for a walk

How can we make a robot walk down a slope?

Balancing and walking on your legs is complicated for humans, which is why the robot in the photo has wheels hidden in its feet. The 'robot' design in this unit balances on three legs and uses vibrations and gravity to move.

What you need

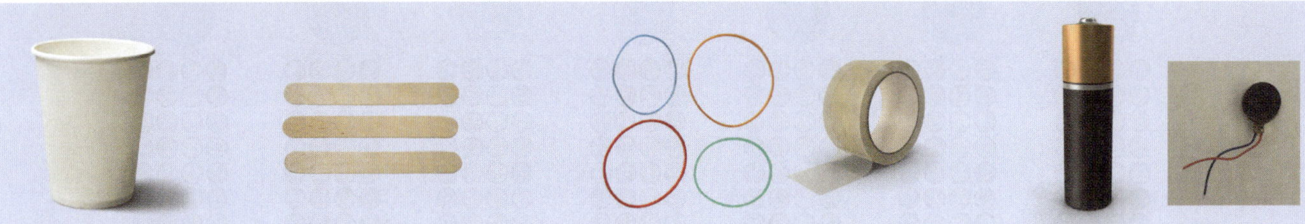

a paper cup

pop sticks

rubber bands and tape

batteries and vibrating motor

1 Attach the pop sticks to the outside of the cup with the rubber bands.

2 Test the vibrating motor with the batteries.

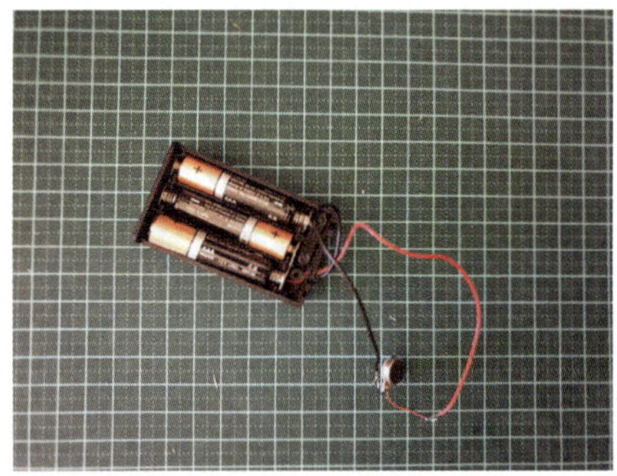

3 Attach the motor to the top of the cup with tape.

4 Place the robot on a gentle slope and turn on.

TARGETING STEM JOURNAL 4 @ PASCAL PRESS ISBN 9781925726091

1 Test your robot on different angled slopes.

a Mark a 'start' and 'finish' line on a sheet of stiff card.

b Add a paperback book beneath the card to create a gentle slope.

c Time your robot travelling between the two lines.

d Increase the angle by adding another book. Time your robot. Repeat for other angles.

No. of Books	1	2	3	4
Time				

At what angle does the robot... not move? fall over? walk the quickest?

2 How would your robot work with more than three legs? Predict what will happen, then test your guess. Would it work with 5 or more legs?

3 Turn the batteries in your battery pack around to run the motor in reverse. Does this effect how your robot moves?

4 Replace your robot's legs with marker pens and repeat your slope experiment. What do you notice about the tracks your robot made?

Bullroarer

How can you make sound using a spinning piece of wood?

A bullroarer is a musical instrument made from a rectangular piece of wood connected at one end to a cord. When spun around the instrument, it creates a 'roaring' sound.

What you need

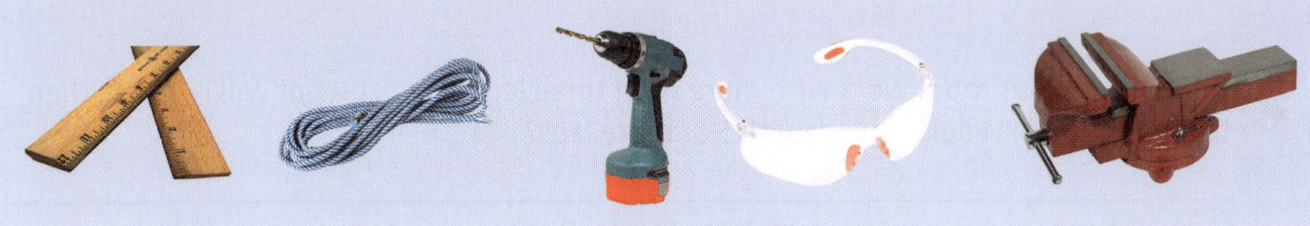

wooden ruler

nylon cord

drill and protective glasses

clamp or vice

1 Make a mark in the centre of the ruler, 1cm from its end.

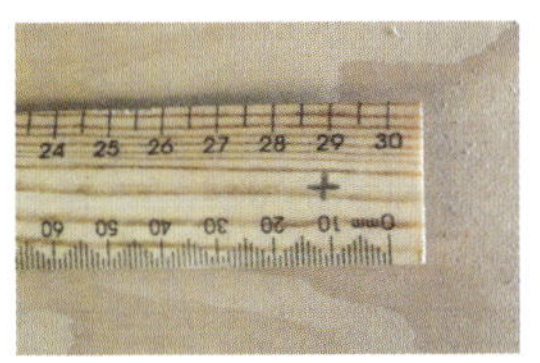

2 Clamp the ruler down firmly. Drill a hole.

3 Securely attach the cord through the hole.

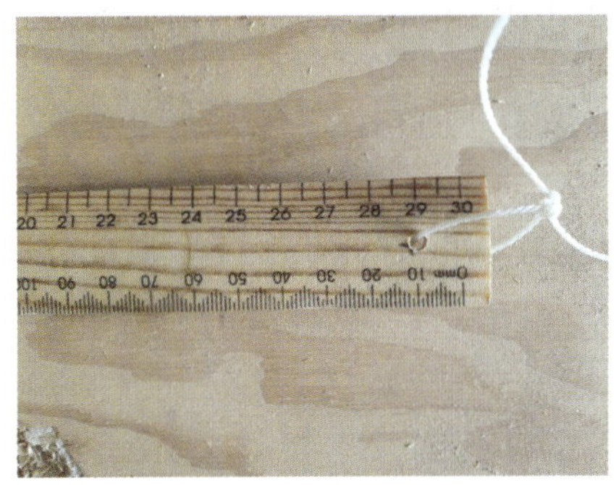

4 Take it outside and spin the ruler by its cord.

1 How does changing the speed you spin the bullroarer change its sound? Experiment with low, medium and high speeds.

Speed	Low	Medium	High
Sound			

2 As you use your bullroarer, the cord will become twisted. Investigate attaching a fishing swivel to the cord.

3 Make a bullroarer instruction manual. Include instructions on how to operate it, how to make it louder, how to change its pitch and safety warnings.

3 Traditional bullroarers have:

- sloped edges called aerofoils
- a tapering body that is narrower where the cord attaches
- decorations

Design a traditional bullroarer in the space below.

BULLROARER NOTES

- In some cultures a bullroarer is called a turndun.
- Bullroarers are found in Australia, India, Africa and America.
- A 20,000-year-old bullroarer was found in the Ukraine.

BEING CAREFUL MAKING YOUR BULLROARER

- Wear safety glasses when using the drill.
- Clamp the wood in place while drilling.
- Use scrap wood under the ruler when drilling.

BEING CAREFUL OPERATING YOUR BULLROARER

- Check the ruler is firmly attached to the cord.
- Only operate the bullroarer in an outside space.
- Watch out for spectators when using your bullroarer.

Frozen food packaging

How can we design packaging for food in freezers?

Food kept in a freezer's low temperature preserves food longer as microorganisms that spoil food cannot grow. Packages for freezer food should contain the food safely, be compact, identify the contents, be cheap to make and assist with defrosting or cooking.

What you need

Frozen food packet samples

Paper, card, plastic bags

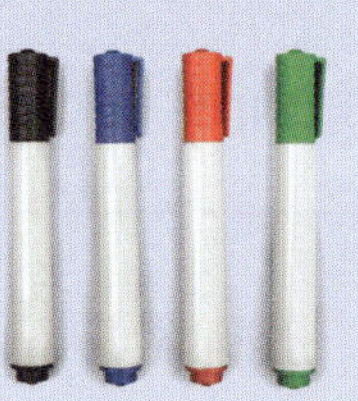

Permanent markers

A freezer

1 Complete Journal steps 1 – 3. Design your own version of the food packaging from Journal Step 2.

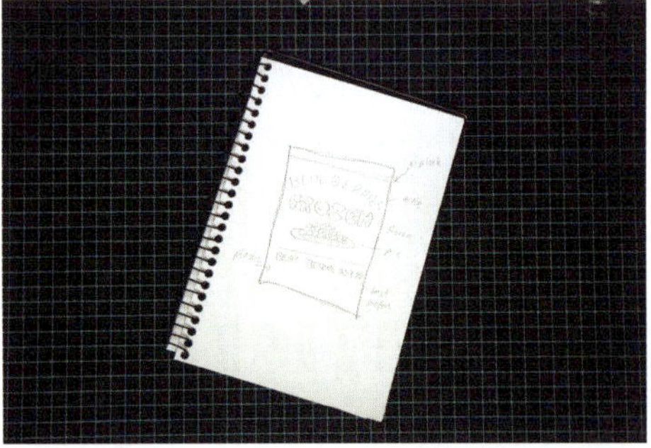

2 Construct the packaging. Keep the inside as clean as possible!

3 Check your finished product with the design criteria.

4 If possible test your freezer packaging in a real freezer. Review and improve your design.

TARGETING STEM JOURNAL 4 @ PASCAL PRESS ISBN 9781925726091

1 Look at the picture of food in a freezer. Does the packaging meet the design criteria for frozen food? Colour the icons (☺ yes 😐 partly ☹ no) and explain your answer.

Criteria	Rating	Notes
Contains food safely	☺ 😐 ☹	
Identifies contents	☺ 😐 ☹	
Is compact	☺ 😐 ☹	
Is cheap to make	☺ 😐 ☹	
Assists with defrosting or cooking	☺ 😐 ☹	
Can be re-used or recycled	☺ 😐 ☹	

2 Think about the materials listed below. What are the advantages and disadvantages for their use as freezer food packaging?

Material	Advantages	Disadvantages
Cloth		
Metal		
Glass		
Cardboard		
Thin plastic (wrap / bag)		
Thicker plastic bag		
Hard plastic		

3 Choose a type of frozen food, such as frozen peas, meat or ice cream. Draw the packaging below and label its design elements. How could you improve it?

Do not eat or cook food that has been in your food package!

CHALLENGE

Chook shed

How can we make a model of the perfect chook shed?

Chickens need a place to live with clean water, food and protection from predators and the weather. They also need to have a place to exercise, a place to lay eggs and somewhere to roost. And happy chickens need other chickens around them!

What you need

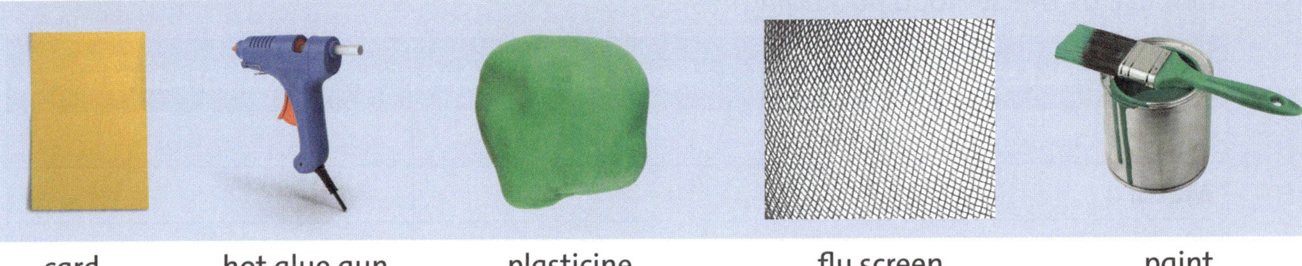

card hot glue gun plasticine fly screen paint

1 Complete Journal steps 1 – 3. Copy your plan to a larger sheet of card.

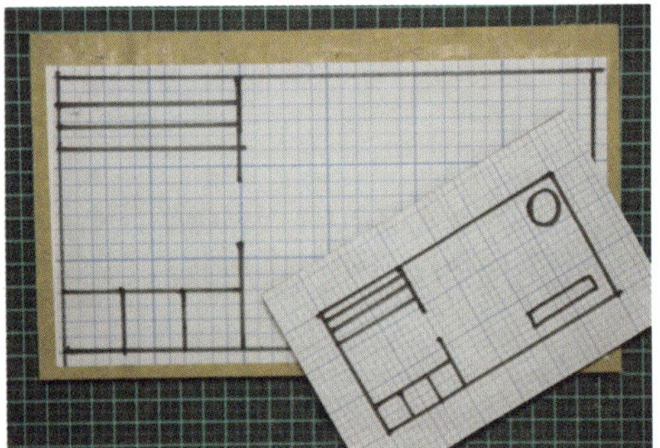

2 Build a model of your chicken coop.

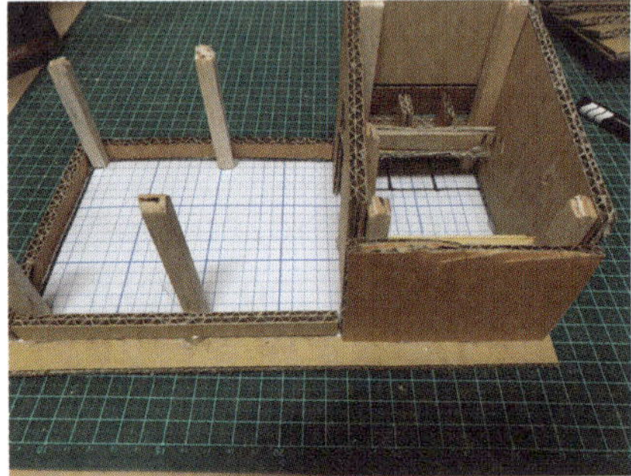

3 Make model chickens from plasticine.

4 Label your model with a scale and the chicken coop features from Journal Step 3.

TARGETING STEM JOURNAL 4 @ PASCAL PRESS ISBN 9781925726091

1 According to an old farm manual, chickens need:

- 'at least 1 foot in length of roosting space'
- 'at least 4 square feet inside the coop'
- 'at least 10 square feet of outside space'

A 'foot' is a measurement of about 30cm. A 'square foot ' is a square about 30cm on each side.

a. How long is a 'foot' in cm? __________cm (roosting length)

b. What is the area of a square 30cm × 30cm? __________cm2

c. What is the area of four 30cm × 30cm squares? __________cm2 (inside coop space)

d. What is the area of ten 30cm × 30cm squares? __________cm2 (outside coop space)

2 Australian states have rules on the number of chickens allowed in residential areas.

ACT	NSW	NT	QLD	TAS	SA	VIC	WA
No rules	10	No limit	6	6	4	5	12

a. Decide on the number of chickens in your flock. Write this in the table below.

b. Calculate the area your coop needs to be. Use your calculations from Journal Step 1.

c. Calculate the area in m2 by dividing the area in cm2 by 10,000.

Requirement	Area required	Flock size	Area (cm2)	Area (m2)
Inside Coop Space (1c)				
Outside Coop Space (1d)				
		Total		

3 Draw a plan of your chicken coop on the grid paper. Each large square is 1m2. Be sure to include:

- protection from weather
- protection from predators
- water and food troughs
- exercise yard
- space to roost
- place to lay eggs

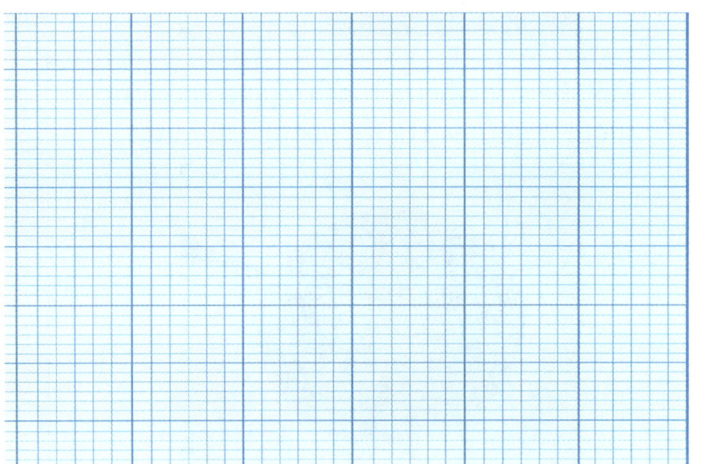

TDEK011, TDEK012, TDEK013, TDEK015, TDEK016, TDEK017

TECH & DESIGN

DIGITAL TECH

TARGETING STEM JOURNAL 4 @ PASCAL PRESS ISBN 9781925726091

Freezer jam

How can we preserve strawberries to eat later?

Jams are usually made from the pulp and juice of a single fruit. The pulped fruit is mixed with pectin, a chemical found naturally in fruits such as apples, which thickens the final product.

What you need

punnet of strawberries | 2tbsp unsweetened natural apple juice | 1 cup of sugar | potato masher | measuring cups | large bowls × 2 | jars

1 Remove the leaves from the strawberries and rinse in cold water.

2 Mash the strawberries!

3 Mix the strawberry mash, apple juice and sugar together. Stir for about 3 minutes.

4 Fill a jam jar and let it set overnight in the fridge.

TARGETING STEM JOURNAL 4 @ PASCAL PRESS ISBN 9781925726091

1 Design and create a food label for your freezer jam. It should include:

- a clever name (4ee's A Jolly Good Jam?), colourful illustration and catchy slogan
- ingredients list
- suggested serving size
- where it was made
- where it should be stored
- when it has to be eaten by

2 Your freezer jam becomes so popular you are asked to supply 100 jars for the local supermarket to sell. How much of each ingredient would you need? How much would 100 jars cost to make?

Ingredient	1 Jar		Cost ($)	100 jars	Cost ($)
Strawberries	1 punnet	250g			
Apple Juice	2 tbsp	30ml			
Sugar	1 cup	220g			
				100 jars cost	$

Research the cost of jars and printing. What would the total cost be? ______________

If you wanted to make $1 profit on each jar, how much would you have to sell them for?

____

____

____

JAM NOTES

- You can cut the strawberries into smaller pieces before you start.
- The apple juice must be unsweetened with no preservatives.
- You can freeze the jam for later.

! KEEPING SAFE

- Wash hands before handling food.
- Be careful with the masher.

WHAT'S THE DIFFERENCE?

- *Jams* usually don't have chunks of fruit.
- *Preserves* contain chunks of fruit or whole fruits.
- *Freezer jam* is jam made without cooking.
- *Chutneys* contain fruit, spices and herbs.
- *Marmalade* is a fruit preserve made from a mixture of citrus fruits.
- *Jelly* (in North America) is a clear fruit spread.

The bee-friendly garden game

How can we make a game that encourages people to make their gardens bee-friendly?

Bees play an important role in the pollination of crops such as apples, pears, beans and strawberries. Imported honeybees pollinate nearly two-thirds of crops in Australia. We also have over 1600 different native bees that pollinate our native flowers and trees. A bee-friendly garden is important to help bees do their job.

What you need

card | marker pens | dice | scissors | glue

1. Complete Journal Steps 1 and 2. Use your template to cut out hexagon shapes for your game's track or grid.

2. Arrange the hexagons on your board. In the example, the purple hexagons are starting points for the players.

3. Add bonus and penalty spaces using the 'bee-friendly' information. In the example, players pick up cards when they land on a bee.

4. Write the rules for your game and play with a group.

To win the game, be the first person to collect all five bee-friendly cards and return to the starting hexagons.

1. All players start on the purple hexagons.
2. Players must roll a 6 to begin.
3. Collect all five different bee-friendly garden cards.
4. You can only change direction on a purple hexagon.
5. You cannot land on a hexagon that already has a bee on it.
6. Follow all instructions on the penalty cards.

1 Make a hexagon template for your game from card:

a. Using the compass, draw a circle on the card.

b. Push the compass point in at the top of the circle.

c. Swing the pencil around to the side and draw a small mark across the circumference. Move the compass point to the mark you just drew.

d. Repeat Step (c) 5 times.

e. Connect the marks with a ruler.

f. Cut the hexagon out.

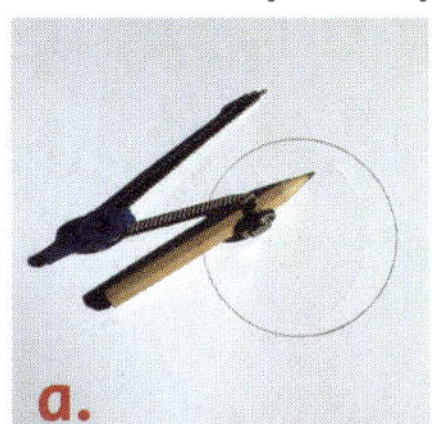

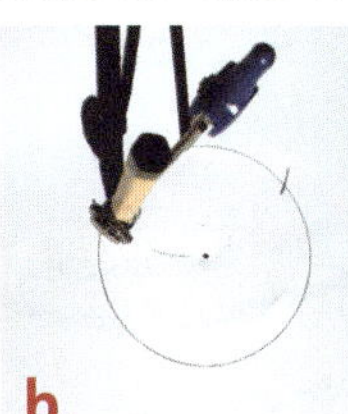

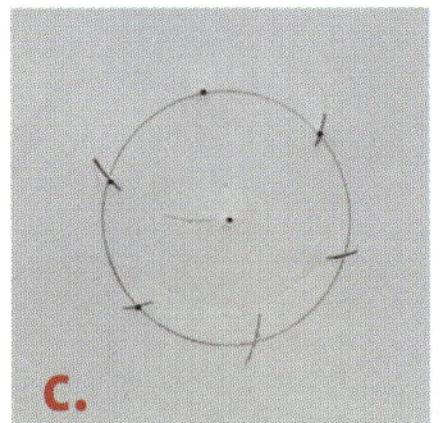

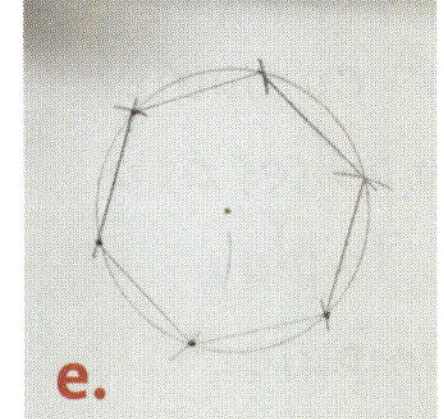

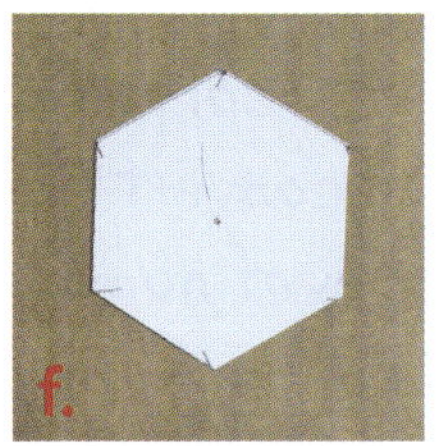

2 Design your game in the space below. Think about:

- The board: Is it a looped track like Monopoly or a grid like chess?
- Counters: Will you use plastic disks or make miniature bees?
- Movement: Do you roll dice or spin a spinner? Are there special rewards for some numbers?
- Starting: Do players start from the same or different places?
- Winning: Is it first to the end or first with a complete set of cards?

MAKING YOUR GARDEN BEE-FRIENDLY

1. Plant bee-friendly flowers such as wattles (for pollen), macadamia (for nectar) and banksias and melaleucas (for pollen and nectar).
2. Make 'bee hotels' for solitary Australian bees.
3. Plant in sunny, sheltered spots.
4. Avoid chemicals in the garden.
5. Plant blue and violet flowers.

WHAT IS POLLINATION?

- A part of a flower called the 'anther' makes pollen. Another part called the 'pistil' leads to the flower's eggs. A pollinator (such as a bee) brushes against the anther and gets pollen on itself. When it brushes against the pistil, the pollen can reach the eggs and form a new seed.

Who am I?

How can we make audio recordings into a game?

Microphones convert vibrations in the air into electrical pulses. A computer can convert those pulses as a series of numbers. To play them back the computer converts the numbers into electrical pulses that make a speaker vibrate.

What you need

a computer or tablet with a microphone

PowerPoint

Pages or other presentation software

1 Start a new presentation. Add a slide with the title and text suggested below.

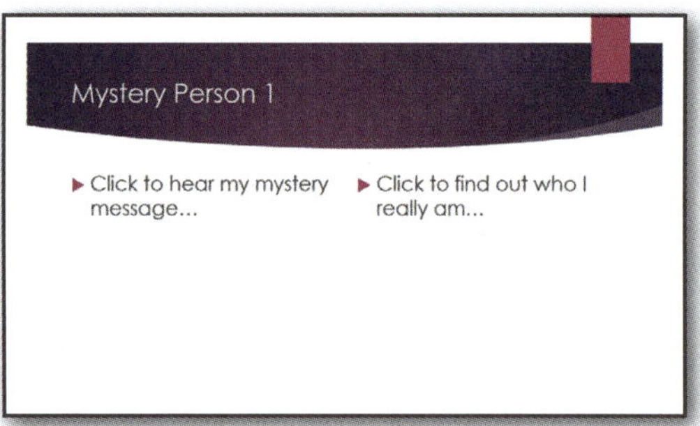

2 Click Insert > Audio > Record Audio. Click the record button and record a partner speaking in a mysterious voice. (Journal 1)

3 Move the recording below the first text.

4 Add a second recording of your partner speaking in a normal voice (Journal 2). Move the recording below the second text.

TARGETING STEM JOURNAL 4 @ PASCAL PRESS ISBN 9781925726091

1 Decide what your mystery people are going to say. For example, they could say, (in their most strange/funny/scary voice)"I am the mysterious stranger from beyond the dark forest!' Write your idea below.

____

____

2 Decide how your mystery people will identify themselves. For example, they could say, (in their normal voice) "Did you guess the mysterious stranger was actually _________?"

3 Add more mysterious voices to your game. Which voice is the most mysterious? Why do you think this is?

____

____

4 Reveal the correct mystery voice with a photo.

a. Insert four pictures of students.

b. Select the 'mystery voice' student's picture.

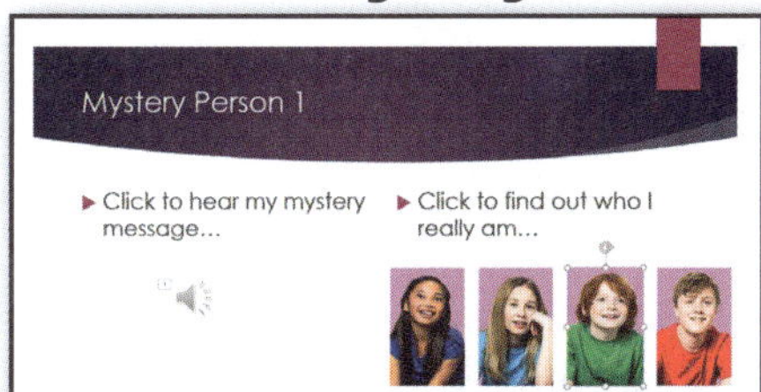

c. Click Animations. Click the More arrow in the Animation Gallery.

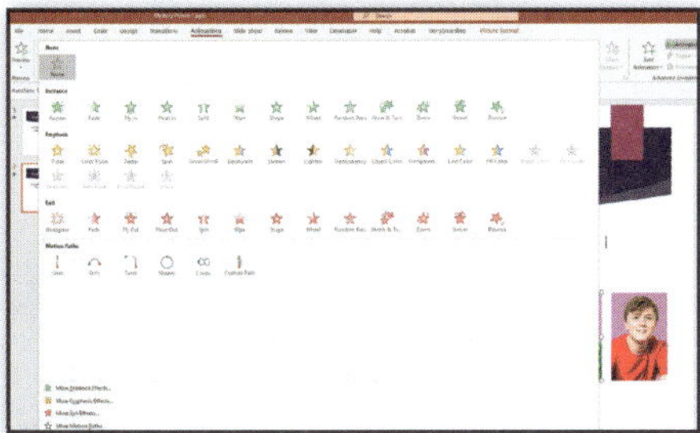

d. Click Spin in the Emphasis section.

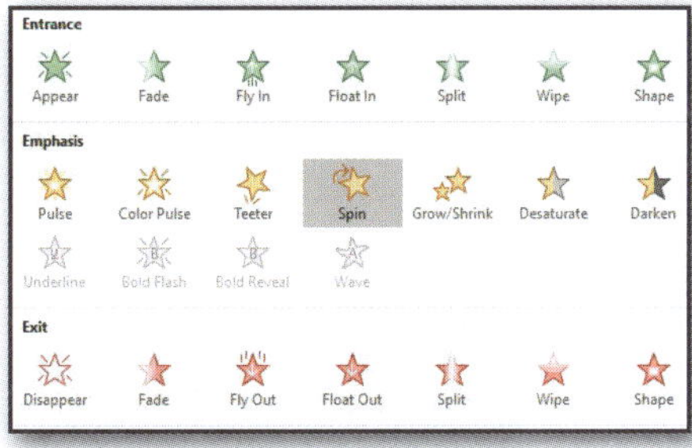

When you show the presentation, the person guessing can click the pictures. If the picture spins, the guess is correct.

TARGETING STEM JOURNAL 4 @ PASCAL PRESS ISBN 9781925726091

Nail music

How can we record and play back a song with nails?

A music box contains a metal comb and a cylinder with raised metal bumps. As the cylinder rotates, the bumps strike the tines of the comb making a musical note.

What you need

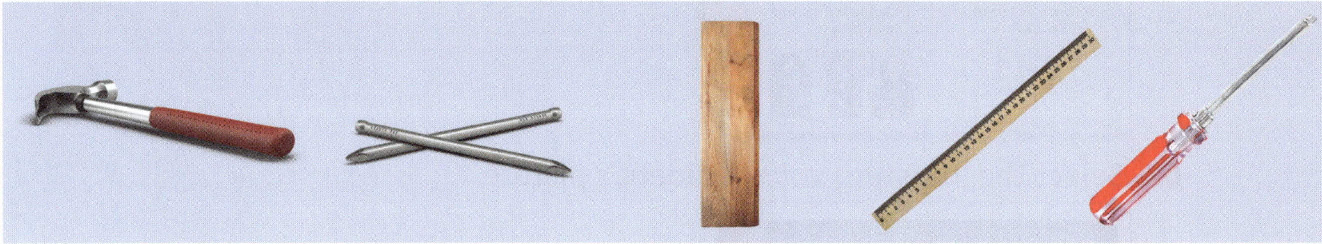

a hammer	long nails at least 50mm long	timber length about 40mm thick.	ruler	a metal rod (a screwdriver will do)

1 Rule a line down the centre of the wood. Make a mark every 2.5cm.

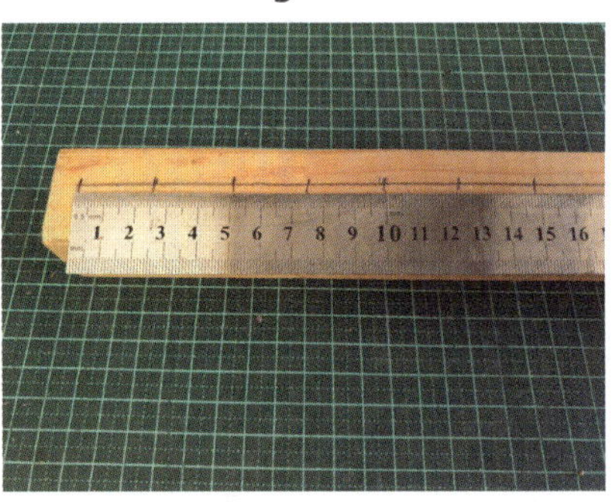

2 Hammer in five nails at different lengths. Complete Journal 1.

3 Complete Journal 2. Hammer in the nails to match your composition.

4 Use the metal rod (or a screwdriver) as a striker to play nail music.

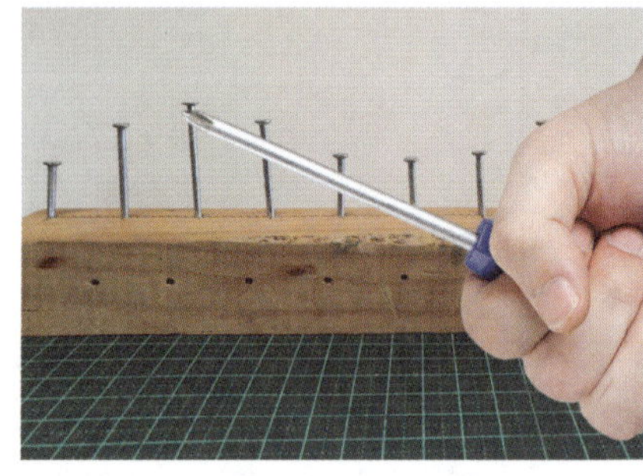

SCIENCE SSU076

MATHEMATICS MMG084

TARGETING STEM JOURNAL 4 @ PASCAL PRESS ISBN 9781925726091

1 Play each of the nails you have hammered in. Complete the chart below.

Length of nail showing	Short	Long
Pitch (high or low) of nail		

2 Create a nail-song composition. Write your idea on the diagram below. Draw the nails to show if they are short / medium / long.

3 Experiment with strikers made of different materials. Record your findings in the chart below.

Item	Material	Sound	Rating
Screwdriver	**Metal**		
Ruler	**Wood**		
Spoon	**Plastic**		

4 Try duplicating a partner's composition.

a. Draw their composition on the chart below.

b. Hammer in nails to match the drawing.

c. Play and compare the two compositions. How accurate were you?

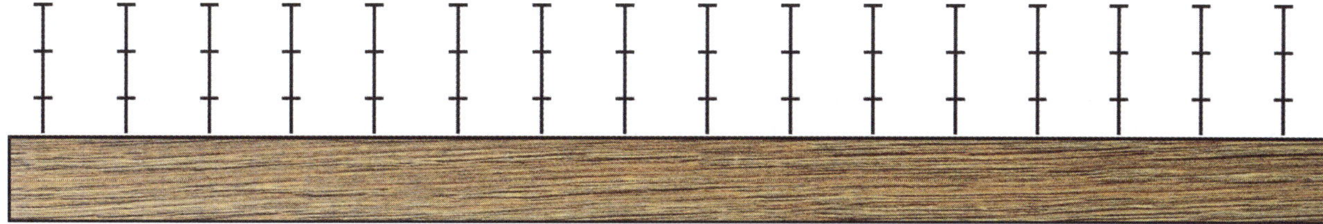

CODING MUSIC

There are lots of ways to record and play back music:

- Music boxes code the music as raided metal bumps.
- Pianolas are pianos that play music from holes cut into paper.
- Records have groves cut into their surface.
- CDs have millions of small pits beneath the plastic.

TARGETING STEM JOURNAL 4 @ PASCAL PRESS ISBN 9781925726091

CHALLENGE

39

Table sorting

How can we use sorting to make information tables more useful?

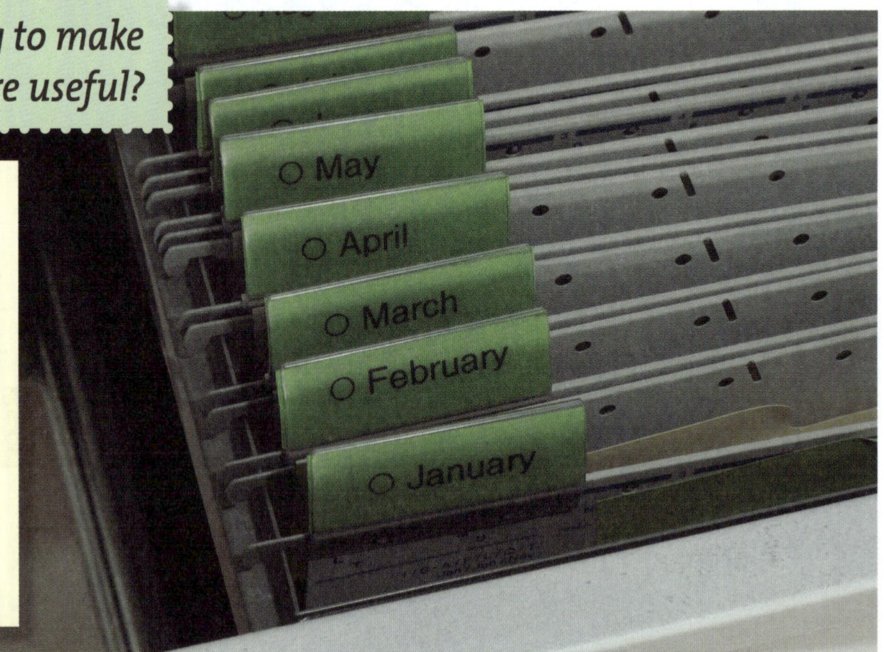

Sorting a table re-orders the information to make it more useful. Words can be sorted alphabetically (A to Z) or reverse-alphabetically (Z to A). Numbers can be sorted numerically (increasing) or reverse numerically (decreasing).

SCIENCE

1 Visit en.wikipedia.org/wiki/List_of_highest_mountains_on_Earth

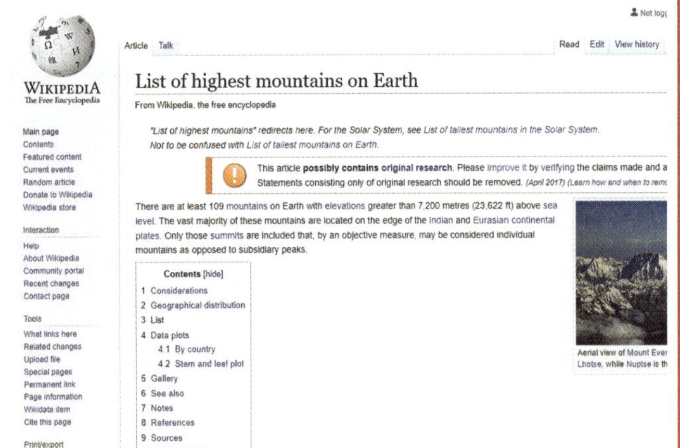

2 Scroll down to the list.

List [edit]

Rk. ⬍	Mountain ⬍	Height[3]		Prominence (m)[4] ⬍
		m. ⬍	ft. ⬍	
1	Mount Everest / Sagarmatha / Chomolungma	8,848[8]	29,029	8,848
2	K2	8,611	28,251	4,020
3	Kangchenjunga	8,586	28,169	3,922
4	Lhotse	8,516	27,940	610

3 Click the icon in the Mountain column to sort the list alphabetically (ascending). Click again to sort the list alphabetically (descending).

List [edit]

Rk. ⬍	Mountain ▲	Height[3]	
		m. ⬍	ft. ⬍
	Abi Gamin	7,355	24,131
100	Annapurna Dakshin	7,219	23,684
10	Annapurna I	8,091	26,545
16	Annapurna II	7,937	26,040

4 Experiment sorting the other columns. Reset the table by clicking the Rk. (rank) arrows.

List [edit]

Rk. ⬍	Mountain ⬍	Height[3]		Prominence (m)[4] ⬍
		m. ▲	ft. ⬍	
108	Lupghar Sar	7,200	23,622	730
107	Singhi Kangri	7,202	23,629	730
106	Kangphu Kang / Shimokangri	7,204	23,635	1,244
105	Langtang Ri	7,205	23,638	665
104	Noijin Kangsang / Norin Kang	7,206	23,642	2,160
103	Malangutti Sar	7,207	23,645	507

MATHEMATICS

1 Answer the questions below.

a. Sort by height. How tall is the shortest mountain on the list?

____

b. Sort by First Ascended. Which mountain was the first to be climbed?

____

c. Re-sort by First Ascended. How many mountains have never been climbed?

____

2 Many mountains have their bases in more than one country. Mount Everest, for example, is in both Nepal and China. Use sorting to complete this chart of mountains that are only in one country.

Country	Number of mountains only in that country
China	
India	
Nepal	
Tajikistan	

3 A mountain's prominence is how high it is above the saddle that joins it to a higher peak.

a. Sort the table by Prominence. Which mountain has the highest prominence?

____

b. Which mountain has the smallest prominence?

____

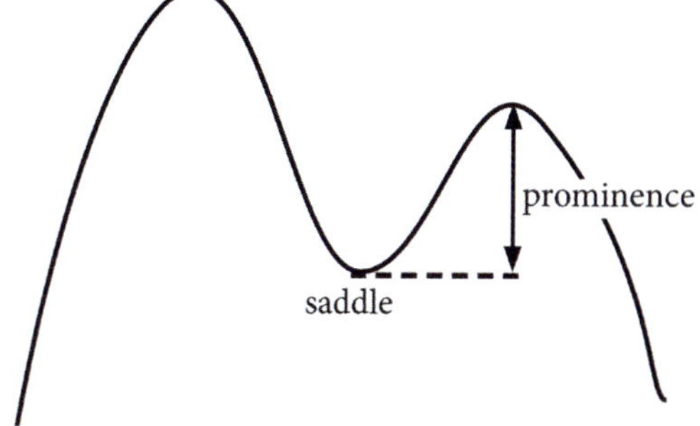

4 You cannot sort the table by Failed attempts as the data is in the Ascents column.

a. Using a spreadsheet program, add the headings Mountain (A1), Ascents (B1) and Failed Attempts (C1)

b. Type in the Mountain name, Ascents and Failed Attempts for the first ten mountains.

c. Sort by Ascents then by Failed Attempts. What do you notice about Mount Everest? ________________________________

d. Why might this be? ________________________________

____

TECH & DESIGN TDEK016

DIGITAL TECH TDIK007, TDIK008, TDIP012, TDIP013, TDIP010

Recycling assistant

How can we use branching in a PowerPoint slideshow to help people sort their rubbish?

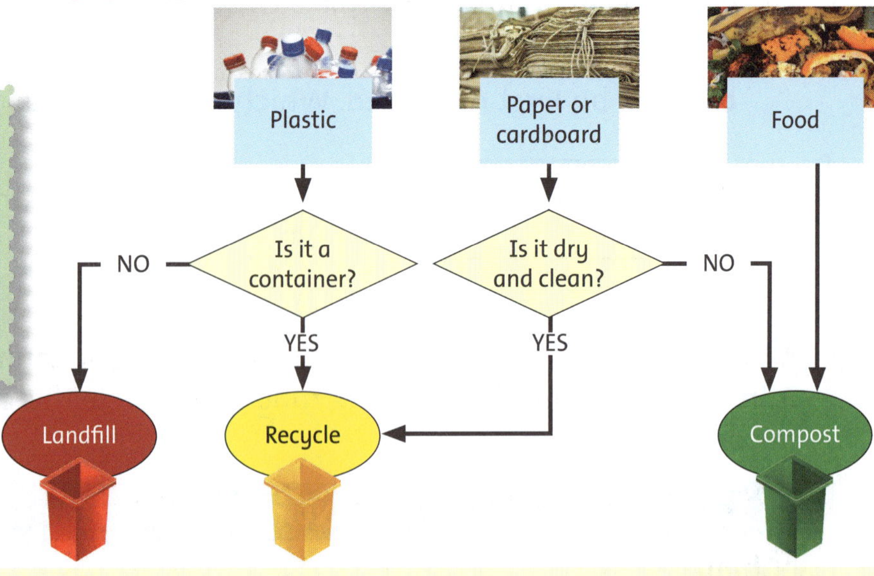

In a computer program, branching take users to different screens according to the choices they make. This program, like the flowchart, helps users sort their rubbish.

1 Create a new presentation and add a slide with a title area.

2 Add four more slides. Title them 'Click your waste', 'Recycle', 'Compost' and 'Landfill'.

3 Insert a text box on slide 1. Type in the text 'Food'. Fill the box with blue. Right click the text box and select 'Link'.

4 Select 'Place in This Document' then select 'Compost' slide title. Click OK.

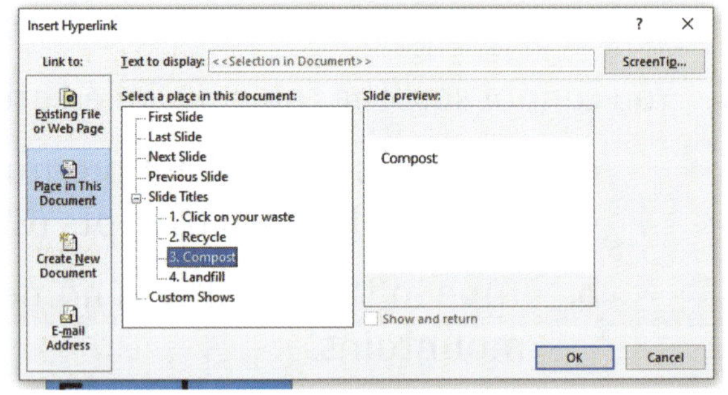

5 Insert another text box on slide 1. Type 'Plastic'.

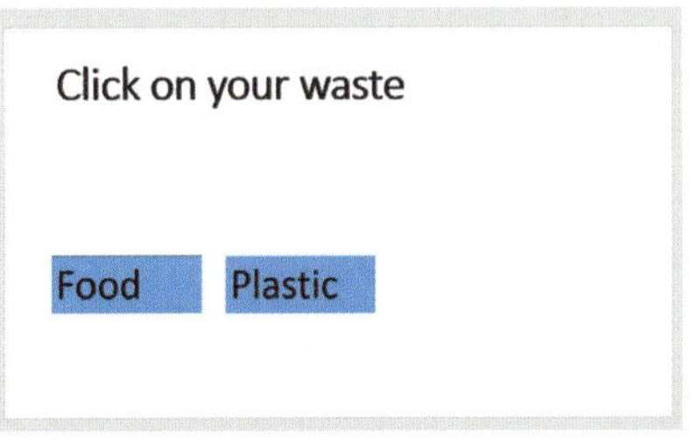

6 Right click the 'Plastic' text box to the 'Recycle' slide. Test the presentation.

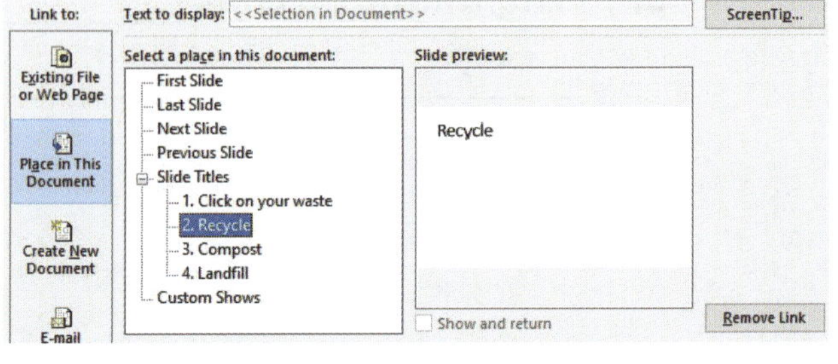

Uh, oh! Not all plastics can be recycled! Let's add a branch to make sure the plastic is a bottle or container before we recycle it.

7 Add a new slide. Add the title 'Is it a container?'

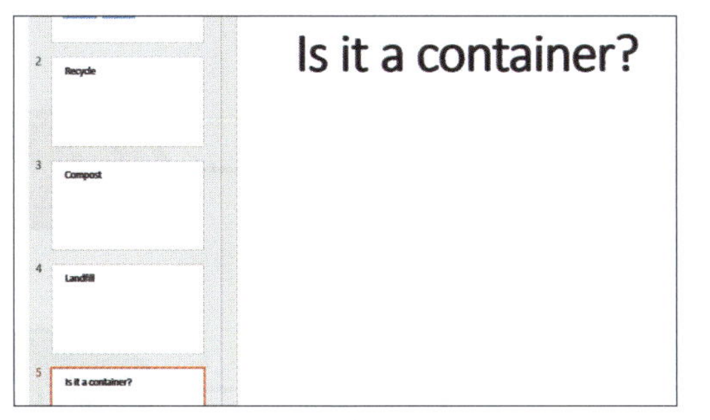

8 Add a 'Yes' text box and a 'No' text box to the page.

9 Link the 'Yes' box to the 'Recycle' slide. Link the 'No' box to the 'Landfill' slide.

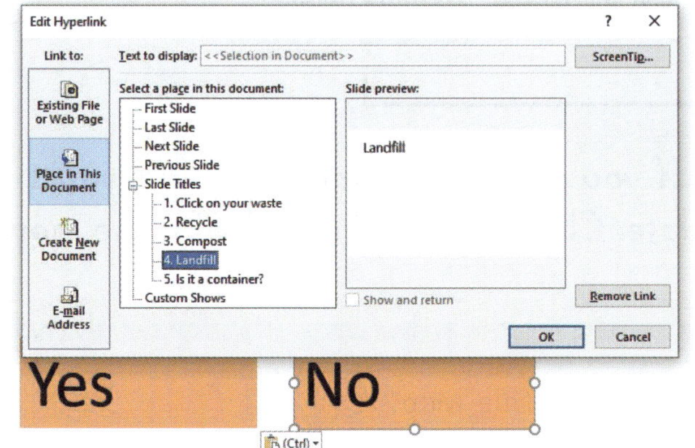

10 Edit the 'Plastic' text box link on Slide 1. Link it to the 'Is it a container?' slide.

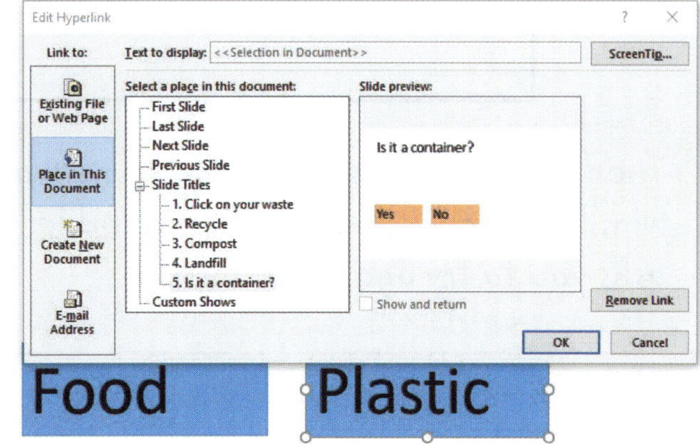

EXTENSION IDEAS

- Add choices on Slide 1 for dealing with 'Paper' or 'Cardboard'. Hint: you'll need to add a new branching slide titled 'Is it dry and clean?'

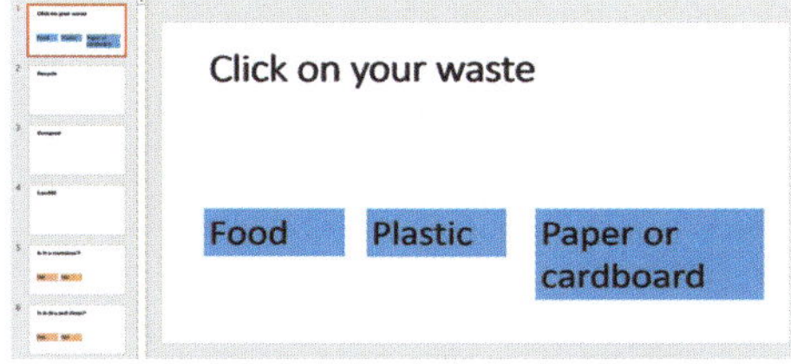

- Colour code recycle / compost / landfill pages. Shape fill the text boxes with colours that match the bins.

TEST YOUR PRESENTATION

- Run the presentation and check that links go to the correct page. For example, clicking 'Food' should take you to the 'Compost' slide branch. Clicking 'Plastic' should take you to the 'Is it a container' choice slide.
- In Edit mode, you can hover your mouse over a link to see where it will lead.
- If the links don't work properly, check them by right-clicking on the text box and selecting 'Edit Link'.

CHALLENGE

41

PowerPoint Treasure Map Game Part 1

How can we create an interactive game in PowerPoint?

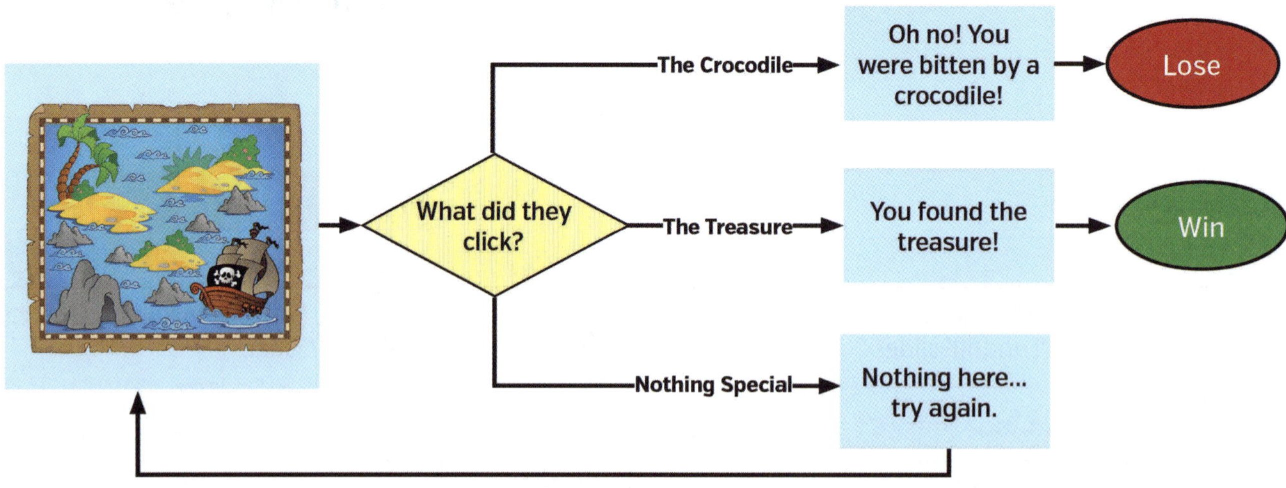

The flowchart shows how the game works. If you click the hidden treasure, you win. If you click the hidden crocodile, you lose. Clicking anywhere else on the map asks you to try again.

1 Create a new presentation and add a slide with a title area.

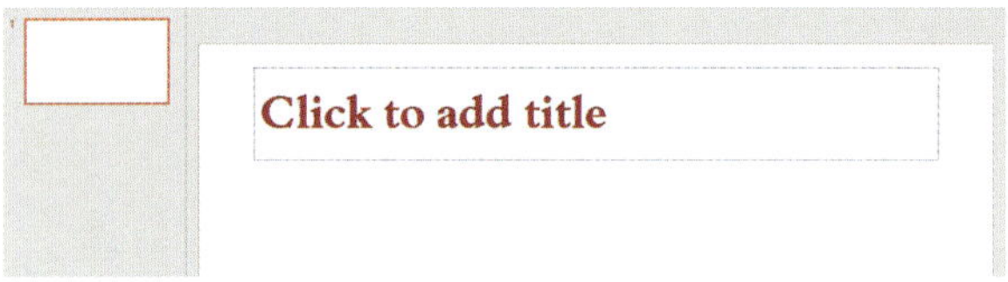

2 Add the title 'Map'.

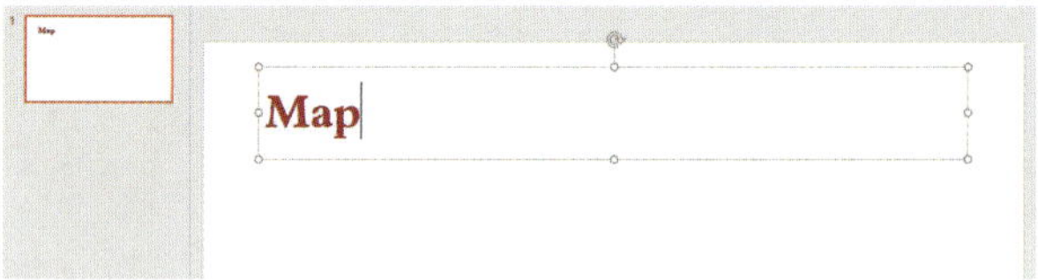

3 Insert your treasure map picture.

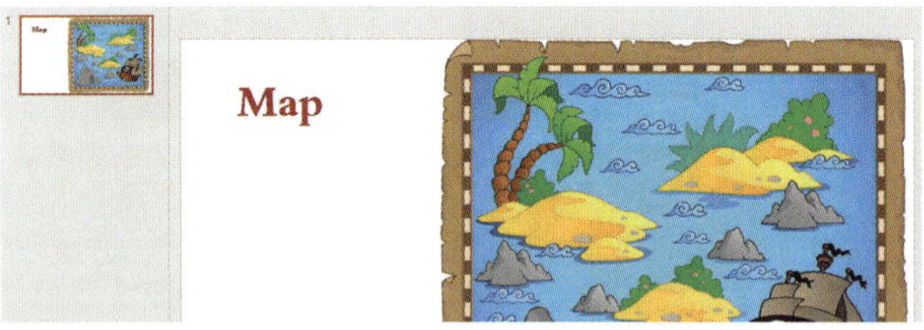

4 Add a slide with the title 'Nothing here ... try again'.

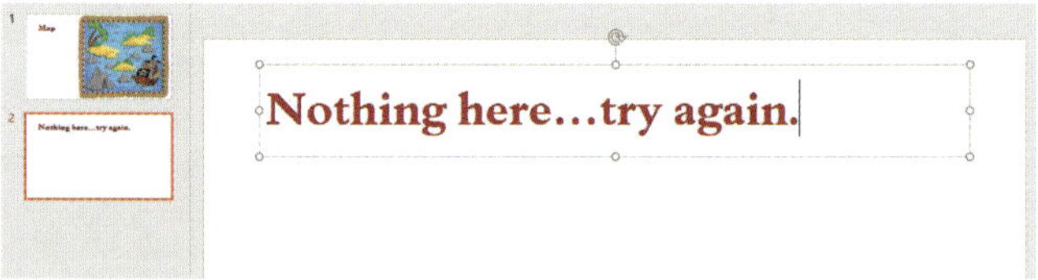

4 Right-click your map and select **Edit Link**.

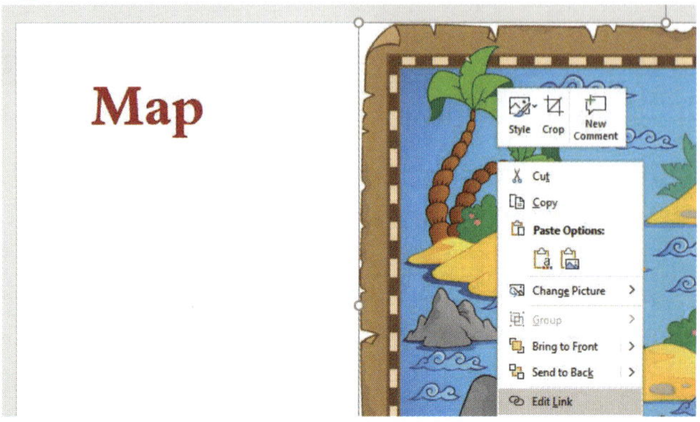

5 Select 'Place in This Document' then select the 'Nothing here...' slide. Click OK.

SCIENCE

MATHEMATICS

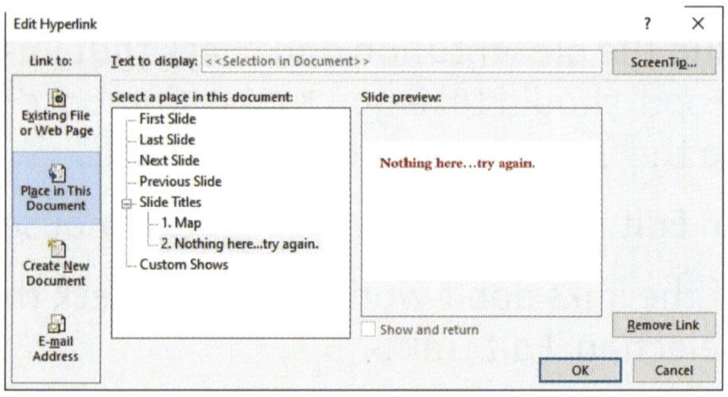

TARGETING STEM JOURNAL 4 @ PASCAL PRESS ISBN 9781925726091

7 Select the 'Nothing here...' slide. On the Insert ribbon click **Shapes** and the 'Go Home' action button.

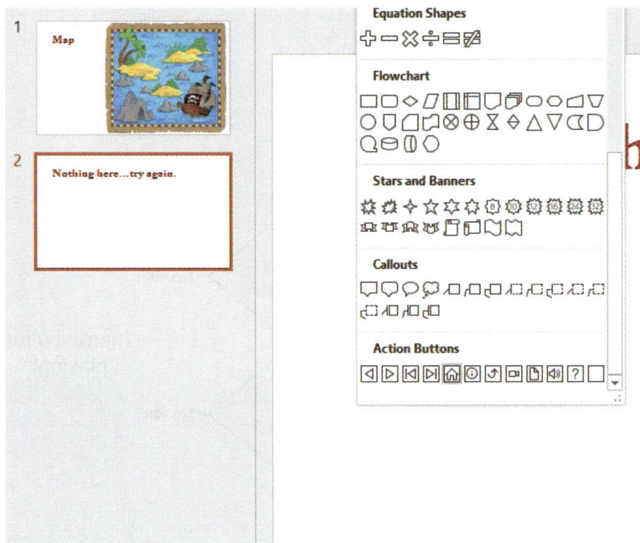

8 Draw a **Go Home** button. Click OK on the dialog box.

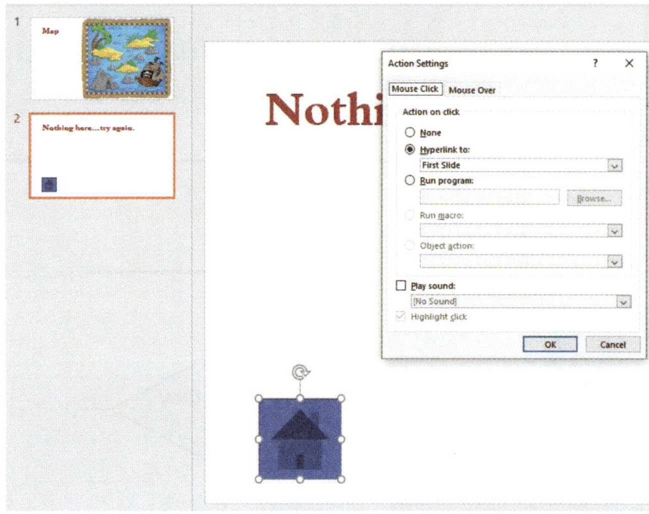

9 Add two more slides with the titles 'Oh, no! You were bitten by a crocodile!' and 'You found the treasure!'.

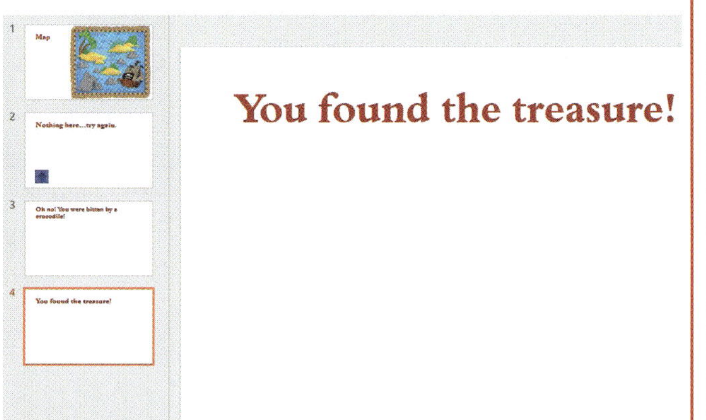

10 On the 'Map' slide insert a circle shape where the treasure is 'hidden'. Right click the circle, select **Link** and link it to the 'You found the treasure!' slide.

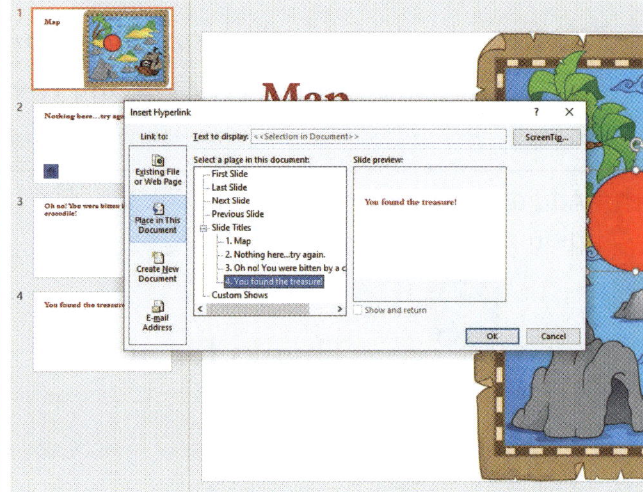

11 Add a second circle where the crocodile is 'hidden'. Right click the circle, select **Link** and link it to the 'Oh, no! You were bitten by a crocodile!' slide.

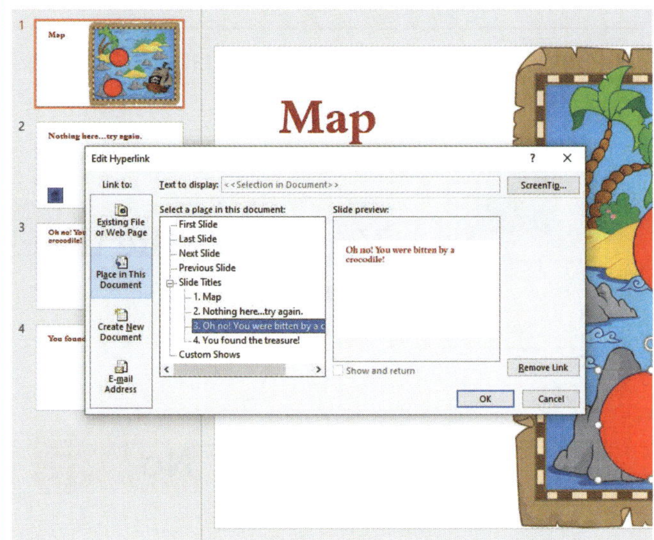

12 Make the two circles invisible by making their Shape Fill and Shape Outline none.

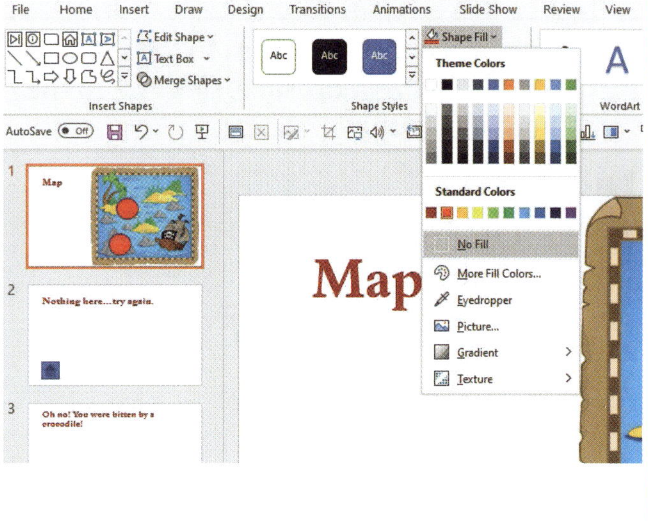

CHALLENGE

PowerPoint Treasure Map Game Part 2

How can we improve our Treasure Map game?

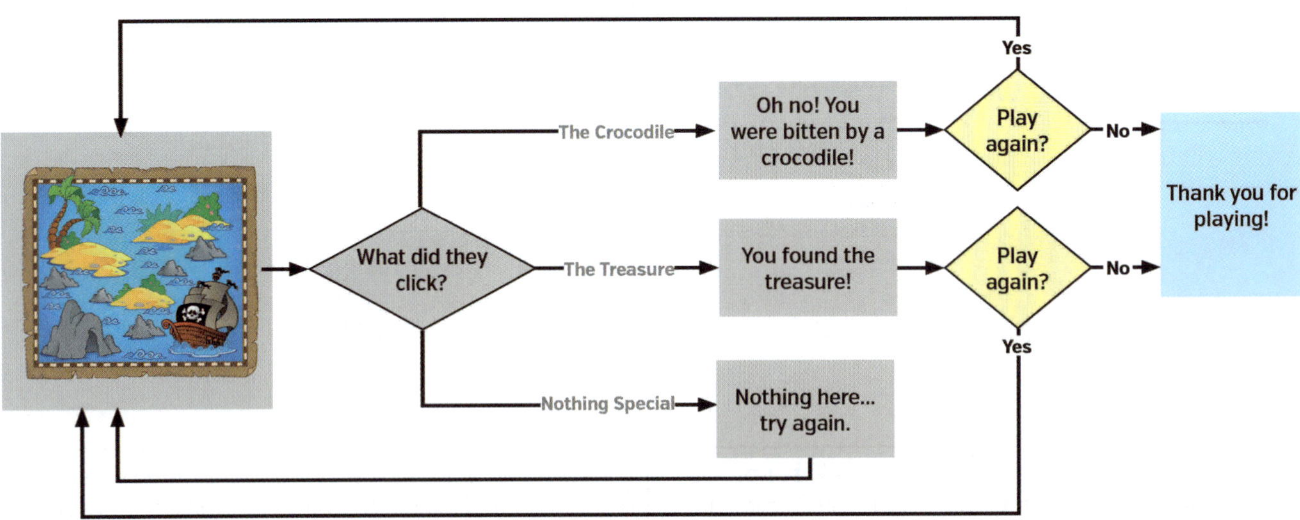

The flowchart now includes choices for the player to start again. If they choose not to, they are thanked for playing the game.

1 Add a new slide and title it 'Thank you for playing'.

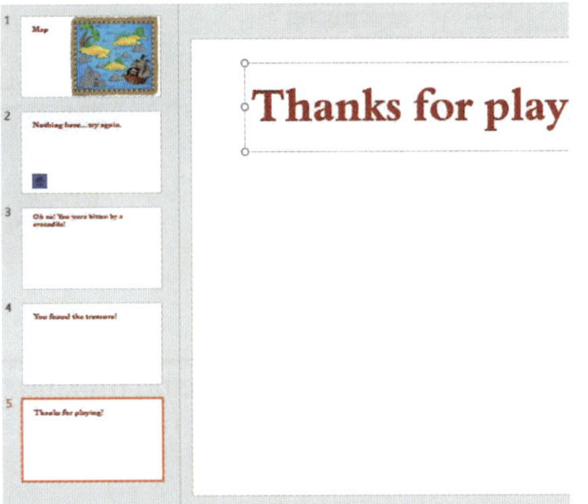

2 Select the 'Oh, no!...' slide. Add the text 'Play again?' to the title.

3 Add a 'Yes' and 'No' textbox to the slide. Link 'Yes' to the 'Map' slide. Link 'No' to the 'Thanks for playing!' slide.

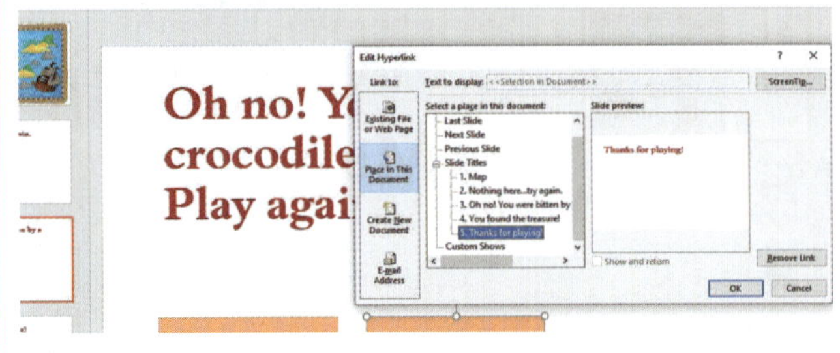

4 Select the 'You found the treasure!' slide. Repeat steps 2 and 3.

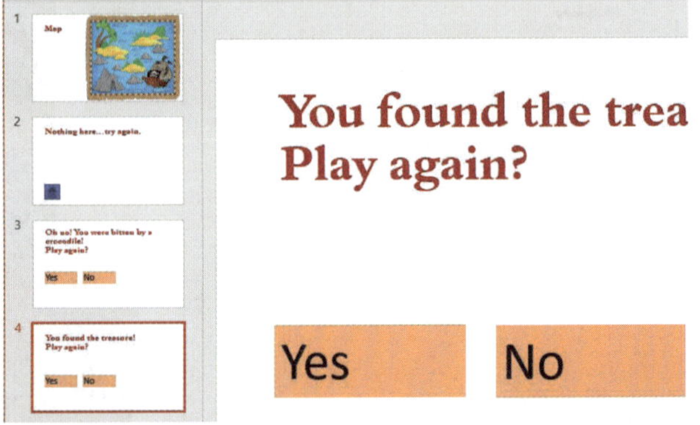

TARGETING STEM JOURNAL 4 @ PASCAL PRESS ISBN 9781925726091

ADD MORE TRAPS

- Decide on a new trap, such as 'Quicksand'.
- Duplicate the crocodile page.
- Edit the title to include 'Oh, no! You've sunk in quicksand! Play again?'
- Duplicate the crocodile link on slide 1. Edit the link to the new 'Quicksand' slide.

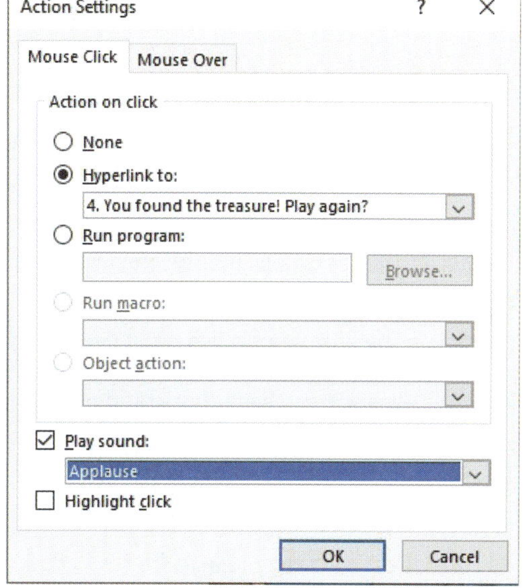

ADD SOUND

- Select the 'Treasure' link on the 'Map' slide.
- On the Insert menu, click Action.
- Click Play sound and select a sound from the dropdown menu.
- Click OK.

ADD PICTURES

- Download or draw pictures to add to the game.
- Add a sad pirate to slide 2.
- Add a crocodile to slide 3.
- Add a treasure chest to slide 4.

ADD INSTRUCTIONS

- Insert a text box on slide 1.
- Type the instructions on how you win or what you have to watch out for.

ADD A SCORE GUIDE

- Insert a table on slide 5.
- Create a scoring system.

Number of clicks to find the treasure	Rating
1	Captain!
2	First Mate
3-5	Deckhand
More than 5	Walk the plank

TECH & DESIGN TDEK014, TDEK015, TDEK016

DIGITAL TECH TDIK007, TDIK008, TDIP011, TDIP012, TDIP013, TDIP010

Note: Answers are not supplied to open-ended questions where students' responses will vary.

2. Frog habitats Page 4

Journal 2: Spin through the air, float through the air, stick to an animal, float in water

7. Growing sunflowers Page 14

Journal 1: Use stage 3 – the leaf has grown from the seed.

Journal 3: Seeds would survive predators if they germinated on different days.

8. Dirty water Page 16

Journal 2: the decaying leaves used up oxygen, turning the Bromothymol Blue yellow.

Journal 3: Decaying leaves use oxygen that aquatic plants and animals such as fish need.

17. Soil erosion Page 34

Journal 2: The rocks kept the soil from washing away.

19. Drain away! Page 38

Journal 4: The bottom of a fish pond needs a soil that keeps water in. Lawns need a semi-permeable soil that keeps some water but still drains. Houses need a soil that will allow water to drain away.

35. Freezer jam Page 70

Journal 2: Costs will vary

39. Table sorting Page 78

Journal 1:
7,200m (Lupghar Sar in Pakistan)
Jongsong Peak, 1930
4

Journal 2: China 21, India 10, Nepal 19, Tajikistan 1

Journal 3:
Mount Everest
Abi Gamin

Journal 4
Top of both sorts, It's the tallest mountain and people want to climb it

TARGETING STEM JOURNAL 4 @ PASCAL PRESS ISBN 9781925726091

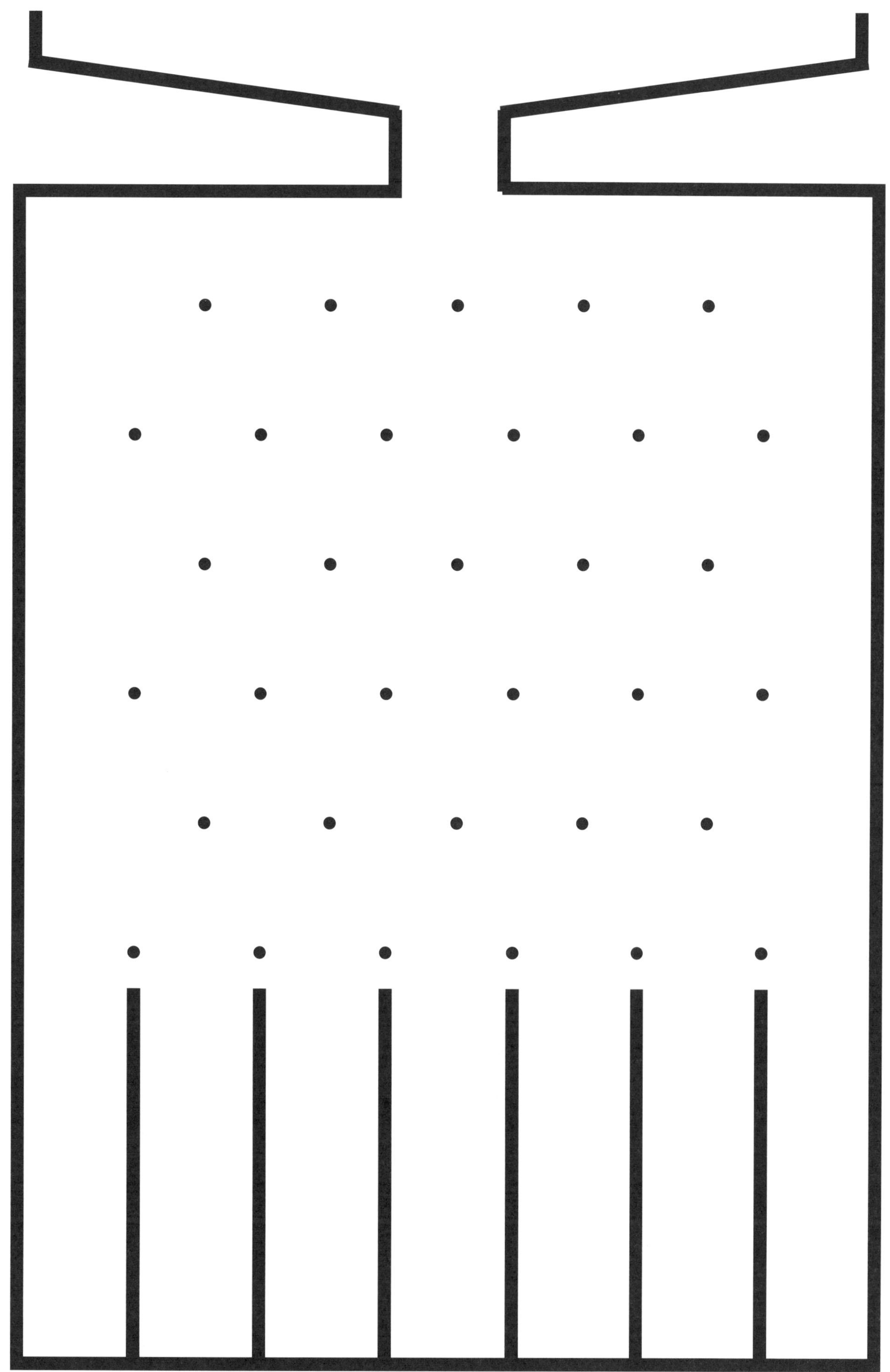

Targeting STEM Journal - Year 4

ISBN: 9781925726091

Published by Pascal Press
PO Box 250
Glebe NSW 2037
www.pascalpress.com.au
contact@pascalpress.com.au

Author: Tim Tuck
Publisher: Lynn Dickinson
Typesetter: Stacey Grainger
Designer: Janice Bowles
Editor: Vaishali Batra
Series Consultant: Narinda Sandry

Printed in South Korea by Prinpia Co., Ltd.

Notes

Notes